I0098565

Running The Race To Win

A Radical Call To Discipleship

By Darren T. Carter

Foundation Publications

www.FoundationPub.org

Running The Race To Win

Foundation Ministries

Copyright 2009 by Darren T. Carter

Foundation Publications

To order additional copies go to:

Amazon.com

www.FoundationPub.org

Running The Race To Win

A Radical Call To Discipleship

Dedication

I want to first of all dedicate this book to all of those men who have ministered into my life and on whose shoulders I stand. It was through their dedication to the cross, which imparted to me a vision for discipleship. In addition, I want to dedicate this book to those who read this and decide to become one of Christ's disciples. Jesus had many different types of disciples with varying personalities and unique purposes to fulfill. It is my prayer that you will become one, who will chart a course for others to follow, as you learn to follow in His footsteps.

INTRODUCTION

Running the Race To Win is the first book in a three volume series **Foundations For Life**. The series corresponds with the workbook **Building Your Spiritual House**. The first section of Building Your Spiritual House is **The Established Foundation** which focuses upon the foundational doctrines of our faith as outlined in Hebrews 6:1-2. (To get your free copy *Building Your Spiritual House* go to www.FoundationPub.org or the Facebook Fan page of Foundation Publications.) The purpose of this first book is to make sure that as disciples we are solidly grounded in the foundational teachings of Christ.

Discipleship is one of those words that can bring several images or pictures to your mind when it is mentioned. To many it is an archaic word with no relevance to our modern culture. Images of a lone monk in the desert are conjured up. To some the word is associated with the spiritual abuse of authoritarian control. I think for many in the church there is just a simple lack of understanding concerning the subject.

In putting this book together I hesitated to use the word discipleship. However, the church must embrace the 'terminology of discipleship', because it is the pathway Christ Himself laid out for us to follow. Since, I will be using the word disciple quite often in this book it is my desire to set forth a framework for using the term. The reason it is important to lay out a framework for discipleship is so that when the word is mentioned we all understand it in the same way.

Discipleship is more than just a teaching for me it is a lifestyle and I am convinced from the Bible that there are no alternatives to following Jesus except as one of His disciples. This book is written out of my personal journey and walk over the last 20 years as one of Christ disciples. As a pastor, teacher in discipleship schools and traveling speaker, I have discovered there are many different concepts of discipleship. During the last 20 years I have walked through what I call the pitfalls of discipleship and to help you avoid the same mistakes it is important I address these misconceptions. I don't like starting a book out by looking at the negatives, but I feel it is important to look at what I consider the three main pitfalls and misconceptions about discipleship. These are not all of the pitfalls, but the main ones that will greatly hinder your pursuit of His purpose.

1) **Discipleship is not following a certain man, church or organization.**

The call to discipleship is first a call to follow Christ. It is a commitment to be in relationship with Him above all else. In what was popularly termed the 'Discipleship Movement' or 'Shepherding Movement' of the 70's, there was a strong emphasis laid on being a disciple. However, within this system of teaching, being a disciple had an over emphasis of submitting your life to a certain man, church or organization. Many of the concepts of this movement are reinvented from time to time in the church. This lies in the fact that there is a fine balance between true submission and authoritarian control. If we are wise we will learn from history or else we will repeat history and make the same mistakes as those who have gone before us.

As someone who has been a part of such a system I can tell you there are many hidden dangers. The most obvious is that if our allegiance to God is based upon a certain man, church or organization; what happens when they are not there? What do we do if the man dies, the church splits or the organization dissolves? What about if the leadership becomes immoral, starts to teach false doctrine or becomes spiritually abusive? The reason I am asking such questions is because they are real possibilities and I have experienced each one of them. I have also witnessed people who had no strong foundational understanding of their individual walk with Christ, fall away from Him because they were built into a man-centered gospel.

A true disciple's life will be built upon the solid foundation of Christ and a commitment to follow Him no matter what the cost or no matter what anyone else decides to do. If this foundation is laid down in each believer's life, they will then understand how to properly relate with other people, churches and organizations, which are all used in the process of discipleship. It is of utmost importance that we keep our priorities in their proper order. Discipleship is first of all about being a faithful follower of Christ and we must keep this as our primary goal. Jesus is the cornerstone of the church and disciple's lives are to be built and established around Him; not a man, church or organization.

2) **Discipleship is not selling everything you have and going to preach in all the world.**

The call to be a disciple will mean that you will be a witness for Christ; however every disciple will be uniquely gifted. In the church only certain people are called and gifted to minister in a country or culture not their own. We are each called to reach others in our sphere of influence with the good news. This will mean getting out of our comfort zone and being a missionary. The word missionary simply means 'sent one' and every disciple has been sent or commissioned to help in fulfilling the Great Commission.

Disciples are called to forsake all and follow Christ, however the call to sell everything you have and give it to the poor is not a call given to everyone. Jesus instructed the young rich ruler (Matthew 16:21) to sell all his goods and give to the poor. He may instruct you by the Holy Spirit to do the same, but this does not make it a biblical command for all to qualify as Christ disciple.

In Acts 3 and 4, we see similar activity taking place among the disciples. What we need to understand in this text is context. This was a specific situation, at a specific time, in a specific place, which required such activity, so that the church in Jerusalem could survive. Many of the 3,000 in Acts 2 and then 5,000 in Acts 4 who had recently been saved in Jerusalem were visitors from other places without any jobs. At the same time, the apostles were Galileans and outsiders to Jerusalem. The apostles and many of the believers were not only outsiders, but also considered rebels by the ruling authority and not accepted within Jerusalem culture. This put them into a situation where many were not able to work for a living, therefore those who had extra provisions like land or houses would sell them and they would distribute to each, as any had a need.

The communal giving of the Jerusalem church in the book of Acts is not a rule or pattern for all church life nor is it a test for true discipleship. These disciples were moved by the Holy Spirit in a specific situation to help one another during a difficult time. As you read through the rest of the next 30 years of the book of Acts you never see this same type of activity happen again.

I am not saying this type of activity is wrong or that it will never need to take place again. It is possible that in certain geographical locations for believers to simply survive they may need to experience a similar type of sacrificial giving. Regardless if this type of activity is ever necessary again the church is to be a community of believers that needs to love, work and share our resources together having a mindset of teamwork.

3) Discipleship is not being a church attendee.

In areas of the world where Christianity has had a great influence, probably the greatest hindrance to true discipleship is what I call a 'Sunday Morning Mindset'. In many people's understanding being a consistent attendee of church is equivalent to being a disciple. This could not be further from the truth.

A disciple is a faithful follower of Christ not a faithful follower of the church. It is estimated that the fastest church growth going on in the world is China right now. Do you think the Chinese Christian's identity is the church or Christ? I can answer that for you because the church outside of government control (State sanctioned churches), is illegal in China. In 2001 it was estimated that the Communist government destroyed over 1,700 house churches. Prior to the 2008 Beijing Olympics house church leaders were put into jail and house churches were destroyed. The Chinese

Christians realize that their identity is Jesus and wherever they assemble together the church is present with Jesus as the head. The Western Church must get a hold of this same truth. I am not talking about a church without any leaders since an effective church must have some type of leadership structure. I am talking about a church, which understands, they are the vehicles by which Jesus is reaching the world, not a building.

Christianity is not sitting in a church service each Sunday morning looking at the back of someone's head. True Christianity is being joined to the Head of the church, Jesus Christ and following Him day by day wherever He leads. The Holy Spirit is not limited to Sunday Morning nor to one physical place.

Discipleship is fulfilling the Great Commission

It is not hard to notice in the gospels and book of Acts the emphasis laid upon being disciples. The word disciple and disciples is mentioned around 272 times while the word church is mentioned only around 21 times in these same books. Let's put the emphasis where the Bible puts the emphasis and rediscover the focus of being a devoted disciple of Christ.

If there is one thing that I want to stress about discipleship, it is that discipleship is fulfilling the Great Commission. The Great Commission is the focal point of the New Covenant and disciples are the vehicles by which this great task has been given to fulfill. Jesus' final words to His disciples included the command to **"Go therefore and make disciples of all nations."** Making disciples means more than just leading people to a conversion of faith in Christ, but includes **"teaching them to observe all that Jesus commanded."** We need to have a clear understanding that making disciples is one of the main tools God has given us to fulfill the Great Commission.

The contemporary church has left the original foundations laid down by Christ Himself and for this reason discipleship seems to be a radical message. However, for the church to fulfill its mission we must once again return to this radical call.

The word radical comes from the Latin word radix meaning the root of things. Radical discipleship is simply a call to return to biblical foundations. Biblical foundations are at the root of discipleship since a disciple is one who has been instructed in the teachings of Jesus. However; the task of making disciples is great and varied, encompassing the entire church. Each person needs to be equipped with a foundational understanding of the faith; yet discipleship also includes individualized training.

The church is pictured in scripture as a body. Although a body is one, it has many individual parts that must work together. Every disciple has a unique calling and has a distinct part to play in completing the Great Commission. Yes, we are all established in the same radical call, yet once that foundation has been laid we need to focus on our specific part to play. It is like when we go to school. At the grade school level we all receive the same basics, yet when we are in University; we focus upon our individual vocation.

The gospel is intended to affect all aspects of our life and even society. It is the responsibility of each member of the body of Christ to use their gifts wherever the Lord places them. It is the breaking down of false ideas that separate the clergy from the laity, the sacred from the secular.

A missional movement applies the gospel to all spheres of life recognizing God gives people grace to serve in areas of business, civil government, church leadership, media, family, education and arts/entertainment. It is nothing new, but large segments of the body of Christ are finally awakening to the fact that we are a multifaceted body serving in various arenas. Bob Briner in his book 'Roaring Lambs' says, "Our job as Christians is not to take over the various communities in our world; it is however, to penetrate them, to be present, to provide God's alternative to evil, to demonstrate Christ's relevance there, to be as good a representative as possible for Him and His church."

Everyone needs to be involved in making disciples. The Lord has commanded us to do so. Whatever He has taught us we are to teach others. This does not only apply solely to biblical knowledge, but goes over into all areas of life. Christianity is more than knowledge; it's about living life. The best way for you to teach someone how to run a business is to let him or her work with you for a season. On the job training is the best instructor. We need to train people in all fields of life to follow Christ and be a witness for Him in their field of ministry. This will take every member in the church having a willing mind to make disciples.

I hope that as you read this book your heart will be stirred to become a more devoted follower of Christ and you will be encouraged to bring others along with you. The thrust of this book is focused on you the individual believer developing a deeper passion to know Christ by returning to biblical foundations. It is not a book on how to make disciples, but a book on developing a deeper understanding of discipleship and developing deeper relationship with your Master. It does not matter if you are a businessperson, schoolteacher, nurse, athlete, computer technician, student etc. you are called to be a disciple and to make disciples

CHAPTER 1

BORN TO RUN

Do you not know that those who run in a race all run, but
only one receives the prize? Run in such a way that you
may win.

I Corinthians 9:24

I was sitting there just watching in amazement at the energy being exerted as the men reached the finish line. It seemed like every muscle in their bodies were poking out as they gave everything they had to win the race. As I watched, I wondered how many hours of training went into this one moment. We enjoy watching the competition while the real work goes on behind the scenes, work that is painful, yet in the end rewarding.

What goes through your mind when you hear about people giving everything they have for what they believe? It is something intrinsic to human nature, the desire to give everything to a cause. Think about it! People will chain themselves to a tree in the middle of the wilderness just so it won't be cut down. The mountain climber risks his life to climb to the top of Mt. Everest.

People are looking for and even dying for something to give their lives to. If you read through the book of Acts then you discover groups of people coming alive with the impact of the Spirit of God in and through their lives. Communities are shaken, churches are started and lives are transformed. It all happened as a result of passionate disciples of Christ empowered with radical mission. Dr. Jack Deere sums up my exact feelings when he says,

[1] "In my opinion, the greatest danger facing the church today does not come from without the church, but from within. It is not the New Age nor secular humanism that is crippling the effectiveness of the church today. It is the lack of love for God, the lukewarmness of the church, that is its greatest enemy today. A lukewarm, loveless version of Christianity may succeed in propagating a little religion here and there, but it will never capture the heart of a dying world."

God has created man with the necessity to passionately believe in something! Why do people spend hundreds of dollars to call a 1-900 number to listen to the latest spiritual advisor? Why do young people pierce their bodies with every kind of ring and put tattoos all over themselves? Why do they fill themselves with mind-altering drugs and go to all night raves? Why do people spend their every extra hour helping a politician get elected? I can tell you why, because people desperately desire to give themselves to a cause. They're hungry to commit to something beyond themselves, something they are many times not finding within the walls of the church.

I have a cross-cultural ministry therefore I understand contextualizing the gospel to the culture you are reaching. However, it seems in the Western church we have removed the root of the message so people can relate. As a result we have many times taken the cross out of our message therefore it has no transforming power and we question why the moral quality of the church looks like the world far too often. We need to contextualize our outreach and services, but we can never compromise the message of the cross. The cross is offensive and the rational mind mocks it, but it is the only power to save, deliver, heal and make whole a perverse generation.

We get a clear picture of the church when we look in the gospels and book of Acts. We see that the disciples of Christ understood passionately following what they believed in and possessed a passionate faith that affected all areas of their lives. They lived on the edge not in the comfort zone.

As I look throughout our current culture long distance runners are one of the more passionate groups of people. We have all seen them, straining and sweating in rain, shine and fog. They give themselves completely to the run day in and day out passionate about their purpose! This is an excellent picture of Christian discipleship. As disciples we have been born to run and it is the gospel that empowers us. However, in an effort to relate we have many times watered down the message of the gospel and reduced it to Western Culture, which some have defined as the American gospel. Eugene Peterson has said:

> [2] "Many claim to have been born again, but the evidence of mature Christian discipleship is slim. In our kind of culture anything, even news about God, can be sold if it is freshly packaged; but when it loses its novelty, it goes on the garbage heap. There is a great market for religious experience in our world, there is little enthusiasm to sign up for a long apprenticeship in what earlier Christians called discipleship."

Following Jesus is more than going to church; it is becoming 100% identified with Him. The apostle Paul in speaking to the church in Galatia wrote, **"I have been crucified with Christ; and it is no longer I who live, but Christ lives in me"** (Galatians 2:20). This was more than just a theological statement for Paul, and it must become more for us than just a scripture we memorize. It has to become the life that we live!

To truly live the life of discipleship we have to lay down our lives at the cross and let Christ live His life through us. This is what true Christianity is all about, but many times we have preached Christianity with no cross and at no cost! I am no way talking about living a works oriented, legalistic Christianity, but the Bible calls for a radical life of discipleship for those who name the name of Christ. It teaches that following Jesus will cost us everything, our whole life!

Radical discipleship is really just biblical discipleship, but it is radical because many Christians have really never heard the call. Let's take a look at what Jesus said to His disciples:

"And walking by the Sea of Galilee, He saw two brothers, Simon who was called Peter, and Andrew his brother, casting a net into the sea; for they were fishermen. And He (Jesus) said to them, 'FOLLOW ME, I will make you fishers of men.'"

(Matthew 4:18-19) (Emphasis Mine)

"And a certain scribe came and said to Him, 'Teacher, I will follow You wherever You go.' And Jesus said to him, 'The foxes have holes, and the birds have nests; but the Son of Man has nowhere to lay His head.' And another of the disciples said to Him, 'Lord, permit me first to go and bury my father.' But Jesus said to him, 'FOLLOW ME; and allow the dead to bury their own dead.'"

(Matthew 8:19-22) (Emphasis Mine)

"And Jesus passed on from there, He saw a man, called Matthew, sitting in the tax office; and He said to him, ' FOLLOW ME !'

(Matthew 9:9) (Emphasis Mine)

"He who does not TAKE HIS CROSS AND FOLLOW AFTER ME is not worthy of me. He who has found his life shall lose it, and he who has lost his life for My sake shall find it."

(Matthew 10:38-39) (Emphasis Mine)

Jesus didn't say pray a little prayer then go and live the way you want and everything will be okay. He commanded men then and He is commanding man today to heed His call to 'Follow'!

George Ladd, whom I consider one of the great theologians of the last century, termed the teachings of Jesus on discipleship the "demand of the kingdom". The demand of the kingdom is not only repentance and conversion, but it must be followed by a life of discipleship. If you look through the Gospels and then the book of Acts you will see that those people who make up the church are called disciples. It is someone who has responded to the call and totally dedicated his entire existence to fulfilling the will of God.

It is Mike Breen who has said, "If you make disciples, you always get the church, but if you make a church, you rarely get disciples." The book of Acts shows large gatherings and small gatherings of disciples primarily in homes, but in both instances we see a clarion call to total dedication to Christ. In Mike's book *Building A Discipleship Culture* he says, "effective discipleship builds the church, not the other way around. We need to understand the church as the effect of discipleship and not the cause. If you set out to build the church, there is no guarantee you will make disciples. It is far more likely that you will create consumers who depend on the spiritual services that religious professionals provide."

If we want to effectively build the church then we must put making disciples as our first priority. Discipleship is more than enlarging membership roles or meeting regularly for religious services. If that is your idea of commitment to Christ then you have substituted human tradition for the truth of the word of God.

The goal of this book is to help you develop a passionate, dedicated life of discipleship so that you can be one who extends the kingdom through your life and helps to build the church. If you put into practice the spiritual disciplines and practices presented to you in this book you will learn how to apply the cross to your personal life. I am not just talking to you about theory, but what I have actually applied in my own personal life and continue to practice to this day. I am presenting to you foundational truths that if applied will help you to grow spiritually and will be used throughout your walk as a disciple of Christ.

God has a purpose for each one of us to fulfill, but we must surrender all to Him to discover His divine purposes. A person who has a sense of purpose is a person who cannot be stopped! Purpose is the divine calling for which you have been brought into this earth to fulfill. You were not brought into this earth just by accident, but God who knows every hair on your head, also has a plan and purpose for your life. He who has said, "Follow Me" knows the way your life is to go. You can trust your destiny in His hands so that His purpose for you becomes your passion.

It is not by accident that you were born into your family, city, state and country of your birth. You may look at your life and say if God has created me for a destiny then it must be a destiny of misery and failure. Instead of being born with a silver spoon in your mouth, maybe you were born with a plastic spoon. Look what Paul the apostle said to the church in Corinth. **"For consider your calling, brethren, that there were not many wise according to the flesh, not many mighty, not many noble; but God has chosen the foolish things of the world to shame the things which are strong, and the base things of the world and the despised, God has chosen.** *"*

I am in no way saying that God does not call people of wealth and power, but Jesus said it is hard for a rich person to enter the kingdom (Luke 18:24). It is hard for a person of wealth and power to pursue the kingdom of God that demands complete dedication, but in no way impossible. If you look at Acts 4:36-37 it seems that Barnabas was a wealthy landowner. We know that Luke the apostle was an educated and cultured man. At the same time Paul was highly educated and powerful since he was from a family who had Roman citizenship that meant they were a people of prominence.

It is a wonderful thing to understand that our *purpose is not determined by our circumstances in life, but by the plan and purpose of God!* Each of us has a different set of circumstances into which we have been born, and no matter what background you come from, there will always be difficulties to pass through. Each of us has been uniquely designed to fulfill our specific calling, and God uses our unique circumstances to mold us and form us for that specific purpose.

For Christians, purpose is not so much determined by our natural birth as by our spiritual new-birth in Christ. In Christ your outward circumstances may not change, but the compass by which your calling is determined points in a new direction. This new direction determines your calling, and if you will commit yourself to a life of discipleship, then you will learn to chart your destination along this new course.

There are many pictures that the Bible uses to explain the life of Christian discipleship. Christ's disciples are pictured as soldiers in a war, pilgrims in a strange land, light in the midst of darkness, but the picture that I want to use in this book is a runner in a race. The New Testament uses running as a picture of the life of discipleship. In speaking to the elders of the church at Ephesus Paul says, "**I do not consider my life of any account as dear to myself, in order that I may FINISH MY COURSE and the ministry which I received from the Lord Jesus**" (Acts 20:24) (Emphasis Mine). Then we see in Galatians 2:2 Paul commenting about the '**fear that he might be RUNNING, or had RUN, in vain** (Emphasis Mine).'

If we take a look at the end of Galatians we see that Paul uses the analogy of running again when he asked the Galatians: '**you were RUNNING well; who hindered you from obeying the truth?**" (5:7) (Emphasis Mine). In the book of Philippians he said that we should be constantly '**holding fast the word of life, so that in the day of Christ I may have cause to glory because I DID NOT RUN IN VAIN nor toil in vain**' (Phil. 2:16), (Emphasis Mine)." Paul's own testimony, written shortly before his death says, "**I have fought the good fight, I have FINISHED THE COURSE, I have kept the faith**" (2 Timothy 4:7) (Emphasis Mine). A life of discipleship is not like running a 50-yard dash, but is more like a life-long marathon.

The marathon is the longest of running races. Legend says that around 490 B.C. a Greek messenger ran from the battlefield at Marathon to Athens to proclaim a victory over the Persians. The runner is supposed to have died upon arrival. It is about 23.5 miles from the fishing village of Marathon to Athens. Today the standard distance of the Marathon is a bit over 26 miles.

The Marathon is a relatively recent sport. It began with a letter that Michel Bréal, a member of the Institut de France, wrote to Baron de Coubertin. Brial proposed to organize a re-creation of the historic marathon race from Marathon to Athens, with a valuable cup as the winner's prize. After some initial hesitation, Coubertin adopted Brial's idea, and the first modern marathon was held on April 10, 1896.

Today when we think of the marathon the picture that comes to most people's mind are the masses that line up to start the Boston Marathon each year. The masses all start the race, but ONLY ONE PERSON WINS. We have each been called to run in the race of faith and Paul the apostle said in I Corinthians 9:24-26:

> "Do you not know that those who run in a race all run, but only one receives the prize? **Run in such a way that you may win.** And everyone who competes in the games exercises self-control in all things. They then do it to receive a perishable wreath, but we an imperishable. Therefore I run in such a way, as not without aim"...

(Emphasis Mine)

Paul was exhorting us to be focused and committed in our walk with God. We have each been called to be a faithful committed follower of Christ and if we totally dedicate ourselves to Christ and His call upon our lives; then when we reach the end of our race we will hear him say, **"Well done good and faithful servant."** Don't you want to hear Jesus say that to you? If you do, then you must **'Run in such a way that you may win'.** This will mean a life of discipline and sacrifice to keep you true to the purpose for which you have been called.

Paul said **"everyone who competes in the games exercises self-control in all things."** Those who have won the Boston Marathon will tell you that it took a life of total dedication. These people have done it to receive a prize that means nothing in eternity, but we are running a race that has eternal consequences.

Do you know that being a true disciple will determine your heavenly rewards? The Bible teaches that God will reward us according to our faithful service for Christ while in this body. That should adjust the way you live every day while living in this earthly body!

If you have ever won a prize then you know what great joy it can bring as you see your dream accomplished. All the hours of training that you endured was worth the price when you received the prize. Jesus finished His course at the cross and conquered Satan, winning us as His victory prize. Hebrews then goes on to say that, **"Now He is seated in the place of highest honor beside God's throne in heaven."** We are the trophies that He has received, and He is our example that we are to follow. The Bible goes on to tell us that we should **"think about all He endured when sinful people did such terrible things to him"**, so that we don't quit before finishing the race set before us.

As I said before, the race of faith is not like a 50-yard dash, but like a marathon. In this book I shall lay down some basic principles that will help you to run the race that has been set before you. It is my heart's desire that once you have finished this book you will be more prepared to run in such a way that you would win your race.

CHAPTER 2

Running Through Enemy Territory

"For our struggle is not against flesh and blood, but
against the rulers, against the powers, against the
world forces of this darkness, against the spiritual
forces of wickedness in the heavenly places."

Ephesians 6:12

The Christian race is not a rosy stroll in your favorite park, but a
lifelong call to discipleship. The race that we have been called
to run will take us through enemy territory. Along this course
there will be obstacles, temptations and persecutions from without,
and a battle of appetites and emotions from within our own hearts.
This race through enemy territory is not an option, but the only way
to run. The course that we must follow is a course in which we will
have to face and confront our enemies if we want to have a
victorious race.

'Running Through Enemy Territory' is the second chapter of
this book because to run a successful race we must realize that we
have an enemy. Thus, the race we have been called to run goes
directly through his territory.

Jesus, who is our pattern and example, experienced the reality
of being in enemy territory from the beginning of his earthly life.
Immediately after Jesus was born in the city of Bethlehem, Herod,
the ruler of his province, **"slew all the male children who were in
Bethlehem and in all its environs, from two years old and
under (Matthew 2:16)."** Was this just a crazy tyrant who killed
anyone whom he thought might threaten his throne, or was he
inspired by Satan to try and kill the Messiah? Herod was definitely

a ruthless, power hungry man who had opened up his heart to the kingdom of darkness and become the earthly tool of Satan's destruction. However, we see that Jesus and his family escaped the hand of Herod and fled to Egypt, because **God revealed to them by a dream in the night how to chart their course through enemy territory** (Matthew 2:13).

Just as with Christ, we too can be given wisdom by the ministry of the Holy Spirit to chart our course through enemy territory so that we won't be stopped and defeated by the enemy of our souls. It is of utmost importance that we develop a listening ear to the Spirit training ourselves to follow His directives. If we want to succeed as disciples then we need to simply learn to follow in the Master's footsteps by becoming one with His word and Spirit.

We don't hear much of Jesus until he reaches the age of thirty. Then we see Jesus coming to John the Baptist and being baptized by him in the Jordan River. **"And after being baptized, Jesus went up immediately from the water; and behold, the heavens were opened, and he saw the Spirit of God descending as a dove, and coming upon Him, and behold a voice out of the heavens, saying, 'This is My beloved Son, in whom I am well-pleased.' Then Jesus was led up by the Spirit into the wilderness to be TEMPTED BY THE DEVIL"** (Matthew 3:13-17;4:1) (Emphasis mine). Jesus was a man of purpose and here we see that God the Father was confirming and commissioning God the Son for the fulfillment of His purpose.

A commissioning is a set of marching orders. The marching order for Jesus was to show the world that He was the sent one of the Father, the Messiah, in whom the promises of Israel would come to pass. Then we see Jesus as the Son of God, led by the Spirit into the wilderness, to be tempted by the devil.

The wilderness is a training ground. Many Christians don't want to walk through the wilderness, but the pathway of a true disciple will always lead through the wilderness. As a matter of fact, you will go through the wilderness whether you like it or not, but it will only be those dedicated and focused on God's purpose that will make it through the wilderness to their Promised Land.

The course the Spirit of God led Jesus on was straight into enemy territory, and every disciple will have to follow the Pattern Son if they want to finish their race. If we embrace Christ in the wilderness it will be a place of growing strong and maturing in our faith. It's only by walking through the wilderness that we learn how to overcome the wicked one and the wickedness in our own hearts. Jesus is our example and we must understand spiritual warfare so that we can chart our course through the enemy's territory.

Enemy Territory

The apostle John, who is the author of the gospel named after him also wrote I, II, III John and the book of Revelation. He was a man with great insight into the very heart of God, and was very familiar with the enemy's territory. In his first epistle he says, **"the whole world lies in the power of the evil one"** (I John 5:19b). Fulfilling our destiny will mean confronting our enemy. We must understand the enemy's territory, because it is here where we will find the hindrances that will try to keep us from fulfilling our purpose.

There are three main enemies we will encounter during our race. They are constantly present to harass us, create conflict for us, and put obstacles in our pathway. It is impossible to escape any of them completely as long as we live in this body. However, we can discover victory over them as we learn to follow the Author and Finisher of our faith, Jesus Christ. The three main enemies that we will face are: Satan, the world, and the flesh.

Satan

It is Charles Stanley who says that:

[3] "One of the foremost rules of warfare is: know your enemy. The more you know about your enemy

– how he thinks, what motivates him, his intrinsic nature – the better you are able to devise a means of counteracting his moves and defeating him. To overcome the enemy of our eternal spirit, Satan, the first thing we must know about him is his nature."

It is a principle in the Bible that if you want to know the nature of something then discover the meaning of the name it is called. A name is given to an object, person, place or thing to describe what it is and how it functions. The Bible describes Satan with many revealing names:

- Adversary (I Peter 5:8)

- Thief (John 10:10)

- Deceiver (Rev. 12:9)

- Tempter (Matt. 4:3)

- Father Of Lies (John 8:44)

- Anti-Christ (I John 2:18b)

As you can see from this list of names, not one describes or paints a picture of someone we would want as a running partner or teammate. Jesus said that Satan's entire purpose is to steal anything of material value from us, to try to destroy our relationships, and to attempt to ruin our physical and emotional health. Satan has disliked you from your birth, **just because you are created and designed by God with a specific purpose to reveal His glory**. Satan is your adversary, and he will never cease to try to sabotage your pathway (I Peter 5:8)

Satan will always be our adversary. He will lie to us, try to steal from us, deceive us and kill us. His ultimate desire is to take the place of God in our lives so that he can be worshiped. His whole plan has been an attempt to replace the rule of God's kingdom with his own.

Satan attempts to carry out his diabolical plan through an organized scheme of deceit. Like a spider, he is always weaving a new web of deceit trying to catch unsuspecting souls in his traps.

Paul exhorts us in Ephesians 6:11 to stand firm against the schemes of devil. The Greek word for schemes is *methodeia* from which we get the English word method. Satan is not stupid. Like a lion on the hunt, he along with the evil spirits under his command, continually works on new methods to capture their prey. If they are successful in capturing your attention and distracting you from God's direction, then they can gain some level of control over your life.

Francis Frangipane in his book "The Three Battlegrounds" says,

> [4] "When Satan rebelled against God, he was placed under eternal judgment in what the Bible calls 'pits' or 'bonds' of darkness. This darkness does not simply mean 'lightless' or areas void of light. The eternal darkness to which scripture refers is essentially *a moral darkness*, but its cause is not simply the absence of light; it is the absence of God, who is light" (Emphasis Mine).

Satan's desire is to blind the minds of people, keeping them captive under his deceptive power *through moral transgression*, or to define it simply, *sin*. When people are living under the bondage of sin their minds become blinded to the glory of God.

Paul the apostle spoke of this in II Corinthians 4:3-4 by saying that **"even if our gospel is veiled, it is veiled to those who are perishing, in whose case the god of this world has blinded the minds of the unbelieving"**. It is Satan's desire to blind the minds of humanity, so that they will worship him, whether knowingly or through ignorance.

The World

As we have seen, according to the word of God **"the world around us is under the power and control of the evil one"** (I John 5:19b). Drug abuse, sexual immorality of all kinds, murder, wars, sex trafficking and perversion has saturated this world, while godliness is under tremendous assault. Millions of unborn babies are aborted in America alone, not to mention in China, Europe, South America, Mexico etc. To continue, I can mention the rise of occult activity, increase of false religions and terrorist activity. The list of demonic activity could go on for pages.

It should not be hard for us to see that these activities are inspired by the evil one. Remember that Satan was placed under eternal judgment in 'bonds' of darkness. It is not a natural darkness, although many times the sinister deeds of darkness are done at night (Ephesians 5:12). It is a moral darkness (SIN) where there is an absence of God, because man has turned away from Him to serve and worship idols. (Romans 1:28)

Satan takes advantage of mankind's innate need to worship since man was created to worship. Today in the twenty-first century, you can go to places around the world and find people up on high mountains sacrificing animals to their gods. Let me take you to a South American soccer game and you will see the people literally worshipping the players. Over the Internet, millions of people worship sex as they download pornographic images on their computers. What about an American teenager who worships a Rock Star, actor or athlete? What about the inordinate affection some give to various spiritual leaders and or politicians?

This is worship because the word worship in both the Old and New Covenant simply means to bow down or to humble yourself before someone as an act of respect before a superior being. These examples are what the Bible calls the worshipping of idols and Satan is the unseen power, which causes people to be drawn to idol worship.

Satan is a deceiver! He is not some little guy dressed up in red with a long tail and horns. In Genesis 3 Satan used a serpent to approach Eve. The serpent was much smarter than all the other animals of the field. He attracted the woman by being such a shrewd and attractive creature. Satan always makes himself and sin look attractive. He comes as an angel of light to lead us into his dungeon of moral darkness. Satan's main weapons have always been, and still are, **deception** and **temptation**.

In 1989, I was dramatically saved from a life of drug dealing and addiction. The chains of death and addiction literally fell off of me under the delivering power of the Holy Spirit. Just months after this powerful experience Satan tried to bring me back under his moral darkness through deception and temptation. The powers of darkness knew I had no desire for drugs any longer, so they came to me in another way.

I was sitting in my backyard by the pool on a Sunday afternoon when the phone rang. Just out of nowhere a girl whom I had not talked to for 4 years called me up. Darlene called me up and very nicely and seductively asked me if I wanted to go to the lake with her the next weekend. When she asked me it was like something reached out and grabbed my heart. I could see a picture in my mind, and knew immediately it meant I was going to be able to have easy sex. I felt paralyzed. I knew I should say no, but all I could say was I would call her later.

At church service that night during praise and worship my soul was in spiritual warfare. I struggled with that temptation until God gave me the discernment and the strength to resist this attack of the evil one. As a new convert I realized that spiritual warfare was a reality and that every decision we make regarding sin will affect the direction that we run. I have not always succeeded in discerning and rejecting temptation as I have been on my journey, but God has always been faithful to help me even in my weaknesses.

Satan was able to convince Eve, through his subtle and cunning speech that what was forbidden by God, would be good for her. We see here that just as Lucifer's original choice to do his own thing had drastic results, so did the choices of the original man and woman.

God had told Adam and his wife, that on the day they ate of the fruit from the Tree of the knowledge of good and evil, they would die. We don't see the man and woman fall over and die after eating, but *the death that God promised surely set in upon them immediately*. We need to always remember that there is a price to pay for sin, and that price is spiritual death. They didn't die physically at that moment, but spiritually because of their independent choice. By that act of disobedience Adam not only died spiritually, but he also abdicated his authority to Satan and was separated from God.

Adam was originally given authority over the earth, but he delivered it into Satan's hands when he disobeyed God's commandment. This left a spiritual vacuum into which Satan could set up his own authority and continue to deceive. That's when Satan became the 'god of this world'.

In II Corinthians 4:4 Paul describes Satan as the 'god of this age' who is always trying to blind people to the truth of God's love, grace and saving power. This has been an age long battle which continues up to the present time. The devil through this world system that is governed by demonic powers tries to dictate the way man thinks and acts, attempting to determine his eternal destiny.

When Satan was cast out of heaven and down to the earth, it doesn't mean that he became limited to the physical earth, because he is not a material being, but rather a spirit being. In the Bible, the word heavenlies includes three levels.

In II Corinthians 12:2 Paul speaks of the *third heaven*. The third heaven is beyond our physical reality and the eternal dwelling place of God where His throne is located. It is surrounded by uncountable myriads of angels (Hebrews 12:22b) who are worshipping Him always and obeying His instructions. Jesus is also in Heaven at the right hand of God (Heb. 1:3; 4:14;John 14:2,3).

The kingdom of heaven is also present in the person of the Holy Spirit (Romans 14:17) and we are told to pray that God's will be done on earth as it is in heaven (Matthew 6:10). It is His ultimate desire to transform this present creation (Romans 8:21) and eventually bring a "new heavens and a new earth, in which righteousness dwells" (II Peter 3:13).

The *second heaven* is what we call outer space, the region where the stars, sun, moon and planets abide. Then we have the *first heaven, which* is the consciousness that surrounds the earth. *It is from the first heavenly realm that Satan has set himself up as 'god of this age' to try and dictate to the consciousness of mankind.*

Ephesians 2:2 says that Satan is the **"prince of the power of the air."** He operates in the realm that immediately surrounds the consciousness of mankind, which the Bible calls the 'heavenlies'. His goal is to corrupt and control the mind of man through a masterfully woven scheme of deceit. It doesn't matter if you are in New York City or the Amazon forest, Satan has set up a blanket of deception to try and blind your understanding to the liberating truth of the gospel.

It is evident that since the time of the early church, and especially with our modern flood of information the battle has increased tremendously. The continuous stream of information in our entertainment society and the introduction of the Internet make the scope of the battle much more intense for the affections of man. Richard Lovelace in his classic study *Dynamics of Spiritual Life*, sums up the world in its negative sense as "the total system of corporate flesh operating on earth under satanic control, with all its incentives of reward, its characteristic patterns of behavior and its antichristian structures, methods, goals and ideologies."

The Flesh

The third enemy that we want to look at is the flesh. Satan and the world can be termed enemies from without, who come against us through the avenue of persecution, deception, temptation and all types of assaults. However, the flesh is where the rubber meets the road. Discipleship is a pathway of learning how to deal with the flesh.

What is the flesh? As we look at the Bible we will soon discover that many times in scripture the word flesh is not necessarily referring to our physical body. You have to look at the context in which the word is being used to determine if it is referring merely to our human body (II Corinthians 7:1), outward ordinances of the Mosaic Law (Galatians 3:3) or man living independent of the redeeming work of Christ (Romans 8:8).

The Gnostics were a heretical group during the first century, which taught a false concept concerning the makeup of man and the material world. John the apostle, in his gospel and epistle confronted the false doctrine that the material world is evil.

Gnosticism had many variations, but it basically taught that anything that was material was evil, yet everything of the spirit was good, therefore Jesus could not have come in a human body (I John 4:2). The practical result of this doctrine in the early church and today is that you have to either give in to the unrestrained cravings of our unredeemed bodies since we are powerless to overcome, or live as an ascetic monk to brutalize the body, bringing it into subjection since to enjoy the material world is evil.

In this book I will be addressing the make up of man and how we are to view this present age. I am attempting to take a holistic approach, which recognizes that although this age has been corrupted by sin and is under satanic control we are not to live lives detached from creation. Jesus came to redeem not just mankind, but eventually even the creation itself (Romans 8:19-21).

We are to live in this world, which means we can enjoy ourselves without being subject to idolizing its pleasures, power and corrupting practices. Spirituality is not detaching ourselves from life's experiences or withdrawing from our communities. We are to affirm creation by finding a sense of holiness in the here and now without having divisions between the sacred and secular in our lives.

The makeup of man is debated in modern Psychology, but it really is an ancient debate. Author Marvin R. Wilson says, "in Hebraic thought, 'soul' or 'spirit' refers to the whole person or individual as a living being." I do teach the tri-unity of man being made up of spirit-soul-body, but not that our makeup is somehow detached and dualistic. Man is one whole unit and we are to function as a person wholly living to God.

The whole purpose of the coming of Christ was to bring redemption to man and creation, which have both been marred by sin. What I am addressing in this section is more about how sin or the flesh affects our walk and fellowship with God. We need to fully understand these areas so that we can learn how to cooperate with the Spirit's work restoring us into our full redemption found in the work of Christ and live victorious over sins power.

William Barclay, who is a recognized Greek scholar, wrote a book called *"Flesh and Spirit"*. In a section called 'The Enemy In The Soul', he examines the way Paul uses the Greek word *sarx*, which is translated "flesh". Paul views the *sarx* as the greatest enemy in the battle for the soul. Barclay gives several uses of the Greek word *sarx* (flesh).

> [5] "The flesh is the great enemy of the good life, and of the Christian life. If we take this as a general statement, then it is exactly here that we see the difference between *soma* and *sarx*, body and flesh. The body can become the instrument of the service and glory of God – the flesh cannot. The body can be purified and even glorified – the flesh must be eliminated and eradicated. It is with the flesh that a man serves the law of sin (Rm. 7:25). The flesh cannot please God (Rm. 8:8). Worse than that, the flesh is essentially hostile to God (Rm. 8:7)."

The flesh is simply man living independent of God. The Phillips Translation calls the flesh the 'unspiritual nature'. The Weust translation calls the flesh the 'sin nature'. The Weymouth Translation says it is the 'lower nature'. I like the way the Weymouth translation interprets the word flesh and when it fits the context I will be using the verbiage, 'lower nature' when referring to living independent of Christ.

Numerous speculation surrounds the interpretation of Romans chapter 7. Is Paul speaking from his pre-conversion experience as a Jew under the Law of Moses separate from Christ or his post conversion experience as a believer joined to Christ? Was he speaking directly about his own struggles or the general struggle of all Christians?

I can only tell you the conclusions I have come to in studying this text and there are varying opinions as to how we should view it. I am not speaking as a scholar, but as one who has studied the varying scholarship surrounding this text. It seems to me that Paul was continuing his analysis of the Mosaic Law from Romans 5 and the believers' relationship to it in Romans 7:1-6. He then seems to be speaking of his relationship to the Mosaic Law pre-conversion in

Romans 7:7-13 since it is all past tense. What to do with Romans 7:14-25? I see the rest of this chapter as Paul explaining his struggle as a believer and something, which applies to all believers. It is both his struggle as a man trying to live under the Mosaic Law (Romans 7:16) and his struggle with trying to live a good life in his own ability (Romans 7:19), which both end in defeat. He then ends the chapter pointing us to our pathway to victory, which is our identity in Christ opening up in Romans 8:1.

Romans chapter 7 is put in the middle of the victory over the 'lower nature' so clearly portrayed in Romans 6 and Romans 8. It does show us the struggle we will face in this age, which Paul clearly shows us in other text like Galatians 5:17, I Corinthians 9:27, Romans 8:13 and Romans 13:14. However, we can find complete liberty and freedom from sin by embracing the all sufficiency of the cross. Freedom is only found in complete surrender to the finished work of Christ and joining our faith into the grace freely bestowed upon us.

Romans 6:12 talks about sin reigning in our body. Our bodies are unredeemed, but not sinful. However, if we fail to reckon ourselves crucified with Christ then our bodies can become the vehicle by which the 'lower nature' dominates us. If we allow this to happen then the 'works of the flesh' can have a detrimental affect upon our lives (Galatians 5:19-21).

To understand the way man wound up in this condition let's go back to the beginning of man's existence. In Genesis 2:7 it says **"the Lord God formed a man's body from the dust of the ground and breathed into it the breath of life. And the man became a living person or soul"** (New Living Translation).

The Hebrew word for breath is the same word for spirit. God took from the dust of the ground and we might say as a potter makes a clay jar; He formed man's body. Then He took this jar or body and filled it with His very own breath of life. The result was that Adam became a 'living soul'. I Thessalonians 5:23 speaks of man as having three parts – spirit-soul-body. However, we must understand that man does not function as three distinct parts, but these three parts are interrelated and function as one whole man just as God is one.

At the time when God created Adam, he was perfect and in direct contact with Him. It was not until after Adam and his wife partook of the Tree of the Knowledge of Good and Evil, that they had a problem with the flesh.

The *first result* to the man and woman's disobedience was that they became spiritually dead and were separated from the Spirit of God because of their sin. The *second result* was that they broke the harmony between spirit, soul and body, and began to be ruled by the 'lower nature'.

According to Ephesians 2:11 the 'lower nature' influences the soul to walk according to the course of this world. In Peter's epistle he describes it as our 'fleshly lusts' that wage war against our souls. (I Peter 2:11)

The Bible also talks about the heart. Most times in the New Testament when the writers speak of the heart, they are not speaking of our physical heart, but the inner part of man. The inner spiritual part of man is his heart and *the heart is made up of both spirit and soul.* The heart is the seat of soulical life (spirit-soul) and it what makes us who we are. As believers we have been given a new nature; identified as in union with Christ and filled with His Spirit, but we can still be influenced by the lusts (desires, cravings) of our 'lower nature' (Colossians 3:5). This is where the very core of the battle is fought, which is the battlefield of the soul. If we willingly yield ourselves then the 'lower nature' can still influence our souls affecting our manner of life and conduct.

This will help us to understand how we can still struggle with sin even though we have been born of the Spirit of God and made new creations in Christ (II Corinthians 5:17-21). It is because the 'lower nature' is not being completely identified with Christ; therefore *sin is dominating our souls* and we live according to this world. We all have the human condition, which is a pull towards sin. Each of us has our own unique make up, circumstances and experiences determining our weaknesses, but true disciples must learn how to reckon themselves dead to sin (Colossians 3:5). Learning how to yield our entire lives to the Spirit and seeing our source, as Christ alone is the life of a disciple.

The crux of living the Spirit directed life of the new creation is centered on learning to totally identify with the life of Christ. This is why it is so important that we understand the core of the battle. As I have already mentioned Peter identified where the battle rages and exhorts us to **"abstain from fleshly lusts"** because they *"wage war against the soul."* (I Peter 2:11)   This is exactly the reason why we must acknowledge that we have been crucified with Christ. We must continually present our bodies as living sacrifices, (Romans 12:1-2) get our souls renewed, and build up our inner man where Christ lives and dwells.

It is interesting to look back to the fall of man in the garden. As we have already seen, God created man's body from the dust and the judgment of God against Satan was that his food would be dust. Satan's food is your 'lower nature'! He feeds upon the 'lower nature' of man, which is independent of God. When we walk under the realm of Satan's moral darkness and become conformed to this world then he is able to eat our lunch!

Through this world system Satan is continually attempting to exert his rule over our lives. He uses deceit and temptation to appeal to those areas in our lives that are susceptible to sin so that he can gain a foothold in our lives. If we allow him entrance then he can thwart our purpose. When evil spirits used Darlene to call me on that Sunday afternoon, only a few months after I was dramatically delivered from drugs, they were trying to appeal to my 'lower nature'. If I had not presented my body to God during worship that night, and allowed the Spirit to wash my soul with a present word from God, then the pathway of my purpose would have been diverted.

Through this world system, Satan has set up many roadblocks to try and keep us from running the race. As we look at the references to Satan, the world and the flesh, in the Bible, we can now see some of the main hindrances to the race set before us. To be able to run the race effectively we must deal with these hindrances. In the next chapter we discover that the only way to deal with any of these hindrances is totally identification with the cross of Christ.

CHAPTER 3

The Cross: Our Reference Point For The Race

"...fixing our eyes on Jesus, the author and perfecter
of faith, who for the joy set before Him endured the
cross..."

Hebrews 12:2

J esus completed His course and ran the race which the Father laid out for him to run. As the days of Jesus' race came to a conclusion it says that he **"steadfastly set his face to go to Jerusalem"** (Luke 9:51, 53). He had a definite destination, and He knew what it held for Him. It meant insults, injustice, the cross with its agonizing pain, and even the Father hiding his face. Jesus did not have the royal red carpet laid out for him as he walked that road. His only path led straight to the place of suffering and death.

Jesus own disciples wanted Him to avoid His sufferings. Peter rebuked Him when He spoke of them. In the garden of Gethsemane His own soul became so troubled, that His sweat became like drops of blood, as He contemplated the crucifixion. Yet, He knew that He had reached His goal. He proceeded to go toward the cross where He cried that last cry, "It is finished"!

For Jesus the cross was not a sidetrack, but the very purpose for which he came to the earth. *For Jesus the cross was the completion of His race, but for us it is the starting place of ours.* We cannot run the race until we come to the cross since true disciples must follow their Master to the place of death. The cross is the foundation, which keeps our feet secure as we run our course. It is imperative that we understand the implications of the cross, because for us to run the race, we must start at the cross.

Knowing Your Point Of Reference

Hebrews chapter 12 gives us much insight on how to run the race that God has set before us. In verse 2 we are told to keep "**our eyes on Jesus**". Jesus should be the focus of our undivided attention. What He accomplished for us on the cross should always be before us and we should continually peer upon the marvels of His finished victory over Satan, the world and the flesh.

Paul said to the Corinthians that he was afraid that just "**as the serpent deceived Eve by his craftiness, your minds should be led astray from the simplicity and purity of devotion that is in Christ**" (II Corinthians 11:3; Emphasis Mine). In the days in which we live, many things are trying to grab our attention and control our mindset. In Ephesians 4 Paul encourages us to not be "**tossed here and there by waves, and carried about by every wind of doctrine, by the trickery of men, by craftiness in deceitful scheming.**" The New Living translation tells us not to change "**our minds about what we believe because someone has told us something different or because someone has cleverly lied to us and made the lie sound like the truth.**"

It is important that we see clearly what the Christian race is all about. To do this we must take a 'radical' look at the gospel message. As I have already mentioned the word radical comes from the Latin word *radix*, which means 'root'. So to be radical is to get down to the root of things, penetrating its essence and not being distracted by the many sidetracks.

Life today can be very complex and confusing. As we have entered into the 21st Century it seems that everyone is looking for some new way. Even in the church people are searching frantically for answers. The path, which we must stay true to, is the path that Christ Himself ran. He is the Beginning and End of our race. Only if we keep our minds focused on a pure devotion to Jesus Christ can we run a straight course.

To run in a straight line, you must have a point of reference. Have you ever tried to make a straight line without two points lined up with a ruler? It is next to impossible. However, with a point of reference we can accomplish the task. A point of reference is something we use to keep us going in the right direction. The message of the cross is our point of reference and when we stay aligned with Him then we will run straight.

Focused On The Cross

In Jesus' walk on this earth, He overcame Satan in every encounter. When He was born and Herod killed all the male children in Bethlehem, God led His family to escape to Egypt. From the day when He was led by the Spirit in the wilderness to be tempted of the devil, until the day Jesus willingly surrendered Himself to the will of God on the cross – He overcame.

The apostle John states that the predetermined plan and purpose for which Jesus came to this earth was to destroy the works of the devil (I John 3:8b). In Jesus' earthly walk He broke the bondage of Satan over many people by healing them, delivering them from evil spirits and even bringing some back to life. However, the plan of the Father was that the Son would die for the sins of the world (John 3:16).

If you have ever been to a play or watched a movie then what you saw was several different acting scenes put together to make up a whole play or movie. In the life of Christ there are several important scenes that the writers of the Bible want us to look upon. Some of these scenes are the birth of Christ, His perfect life, His miraculous power, and His fulfillment of prophetic promises. Yet, as we look at the testimony of scripture I would say that the most important scene that we need to view is the scene of the cross.

The Christian author Richard Booker says that,

[7] "The blood covenant is the 'scarlet thread', that runs throughout the entire Bible. All other teachings are woven into it."

The shed blood on the cross is undoubtedly one of the main focal points all the Old Testament and New Testament writers focused upon.

As the final scene of Jesus' earthly life opens, we see Him walking down that final stretch to the fulfillment of His destiny. He has just been beaten and whipped so badly by the Roman soldiers that you could not even recognize Him. The soldiers then placed His cross upon His shoulders as He began to walk down the road to Calvary, yet He was so weak they made a man named Simon who was a Cyrenian, carry it for Him. He was then nailed to the cross. Crucifixion was a horrific way to die. The Romans reserved this type of public execution for the lowest of society. Crucifixion was used as an example to slaves and rebels who had absolutely no rights in society to not resist Roman authority.

As Jesus was on the cross Luke 23:44-45 says, "**about the sixth hour, there was darkness over all the earth until the ninth hour. Then the sun was darkened, and the veil of the temple was torn in two.**" Then Jesus cried out with a loud voice, "IT IS FINISHED!" I dare to say that I believe that these are the most transitional and important words ever mentioned in the Bible. These were such important words that darkness fell over the whole land for three hours. It seems that all of creation *stopped to watch this final climatic scene of the ages as Jesus paid for mankind's sin and the power of satanic oppression over mankind was broken once and for all.*

The 'Word Of The Cross'

In Paul's first letter to the church in Corinth he had to bring them back to being singly focused on the cross. They had begun to listen to several factious voices, which began leading certain groups of them down different paths. Paul instructed the Corinthians to become focused around one simple message, which he called "the word of the cross". The unity of the faith is established around the person of Christ and message of the cross.

The 'word of the cross' is the **power** to overcome sin, Satan, the world and the flesh, but it is also the **wisdom** to build an intimate relationship with God and others. Wisdom is the very essence of how to live a life of overcoming purpose through the manifest presence of God (I Corinthians 1:24).

The 'word' or message of the cross is the very foundation of our faith. In the Vine's Expository it defines the word 'foundation' as the [1] The ministry of the gospel and the doctrines of the faith. (Rom. 15:20; I Cor. 3:10,11; Eph. 2:20). [2] The foundation laid by God, - not the church (which is not a "foundation"), but to Christ Himself, upon whom the saints are built. There must come a fresh emphasis on Christ Himself.

Paul declared the essence of the apostolic message in I Corinthians 2:2 when he said, **"I determined to know nothing among you except Jesus Christ, and Him crucified."** The apostolic message is centered on Christ. The 'word of the cross' releases the very power of God to destroy the works of darkness and the wisdom of God to build the church. Christ displayed the power of God when He walked this earth and He has commissioned His church with His apostolic power to set the captives free. Not only is His supernatural power released through the word of the cross, but also His wisdom. The word of the cross establishes us on the secure foundation of Christ the very wisdom of God, which will stand through the fires of persecution and tribulation.

The 'word of the cross' is not just a message about Christ's crucifixion, but also of His resurrection and ascension as the Victor. Jesus' complete and total victory over Satan, sin, the world and the flesh is clearly shown in the Word of God. That victory was won at the cross, sealed on the day of His resurrection, and established when He ascended to be seated at the right hand of the Father to be our representative in Heaven.

The salvation that Christ has provided will affect every area of our lives. As disciples there is not an area of our lives which should not be submitted to the Lordship of Christ. When Adam sinned, his total nature was corrupted. Since we are Adam's offspring we have been separated from God and doomed to the same fate as Satan, which is eternal damnation. However, God has provided a way out of the prison cell of sin. The key to unlock the prison door is Christ.

Jesus is our victory, yet the victory of the cross has been laid out in the terms of a covenant, so in order to understand the 'word of the cross' and its full impact on our lives, then we must understand the terms of the covenant.

The New Covenant

On the night before Jesus finished His race at the cross, He ate the last Passover meal with His disciples in the upper room. The symbolic nature of this last meal with His disciples demonstrates the significant change His death and resurrection was about to bring in how man and God would relate to one another.

As He was entering into this special night with His disciples, they were on the verge of consummating the main theme of all the prophetic promises given in the Old Testament. On this night Jesus spoke of entering into a *COVENANT,* or, as some manuscripts say, a *NEW COVENANT.*

Covenant, is one of the leading concepts of the Old Testament. The Hebrew word for covenant is *berîth* and it contains the sense of **a binding** or **a bond.** It also means a **'cutting in pieces,'** usually of one or more sacrificial victims. This word signifies that through the 'cutting in pieces' of a sacrificial victim and the shedding of blood there is going to be a binding or bonding agreement made between two parties.

In our day with all of the animal rights activists, the Bible looks barbaric, but there is a purpose in the killing of innocent sacrificial victims and the shedding of blood. We saw in the last chapter that Satan is the 'god of this world', or you might say the 'god of this present evil age' because Adam allowed him to establish his kingdom of darkness into the void left in mankind by Adams' sin. Yet, if we go back to Genesis chapter three, where Satan deceived Adam and Eve, we will remember that God in His grace thwarted Satan's coup d'état to take over completely.

God set His plan in motion that worked even in Adam's failure because God promised that one day **'His very own Seed'** would come through the woman to crush Satan. This was the first prophetic promise given concerning a future Messiah who would liberate man from Satan's rule and bring him back under God's rule.

Adam's penalty for disobedience was death. This death was to be manifested in three specific ways: spiritual death, which is man separated from the life of God because of sin; physical death, which occurs when the physical body is separated from the inner man which is the spirit-soul; and the ultimate effect of death which is eternal separation from God because of sin. Man's body can die physically, but the spiritual part of man, his spirit-soul, can never be exterminated.

In Genesis 3:21, just after Adam and Eve received the prophetic promise, that one day they would be delivered from Satan's power through the 'seed of the woman', **God covered them with animal skins.** The Bible does not directly say it, but God must have killed an animal or animals to clothe Adam and Eve. The New American Standard Bible says, **"And the Lord God MADE GARMENTS OF SKIN for Adam and his wife and clothed them"** (Emphasis Mine). The Hebrew word for **made** is *âsâh* and one of its meanings is 'to sacrifice'. I would like to do a personal translation of this text and say, *"The Lord God sacrificed for Adam and his wife and clothed them with garments of skin."*

What we want to do next is discover why God would do such a thing? The reason is because God is a God of mercy and holiness. You cannot separate His mercy from His holiness. God's holiness could not allow Adam and Eve's rebellion to go unpunished. He loved them, but He could not be merciful and loving at the expense of His justice. He had to punish them for their disobedience because to allow rebellion to go unpunished would result in chaos.

At the same time, God's mercy reached out in unfailing love to provide a way of escape. That way of escape was the sacrifice of an innocent victim **who took their death penalty and was punished in their place.**

The sacrifice of an innocent victim and the promise of the 'seed of the woman' both found their ultimate fulfillment in Christ. It is by looking at the Passover that we can best understand the blood covenant. It is because the Passover is one of those portions of the Bible, which is a main link between both the New and Old Covenant.

On the night before Jesus went to the cross He partook of the last Passover meal with His disciples, and it was on this night that there was a completion of the old and a bringing in of the new. The first Passover found its fulfillment in Christ and was simply a model of the Last Supper.

Out of all the gospel stories, which tell the life of Christ, it is John's gospel, which centers on the Passover. John's account uses the Passover as a guide, to help us see that in Christ, there was a completion of the Old Covenant promises and the starting of a New Covenant between God and man through Him.

The central focus of the Passover is the sacrifice.

> [8] "It was the Passover sacrifice which delivered Israel from the power of Pharaoh so that her people would never again serve Egypt."

This was the sacrifice, which brought the final separation between the children of Israel and the Egyptians. What seemed like foolishness to the Egyptians was really the power of God in demonstration, to deliver those who had faith in the God who commanded the sacrifice of the Passover lamb (I Corinthians 1:18). At the same time, God's wisdom was seen in action, by the obedience of the Hebrew people to apply the blood to their homes.

Instead of going through all of the details of the Passover as recorded in Exodus 12, we are just going to look at the main points which the New Covenant that Christ established focuses upon. These are the body, the blood, the meal and the new beginning of the Passover.

'A BODY YOU HAVE PREPARED FOR ME'

Among some, there is a debate as to whether Christ partook of the Passover meal or of the Lord's Supper on that last night with His disciples before His crucifixion. He did both. At the same time, it was the last Passover meal and the first time the Lord's Supper was eaten. In Matthew's gospel it says **"while they were eating, Jesus took some bread, and after a blessing, He broke it and gave it to the disciples, and said take**, *eat; this is My body*". **(Emphasis Mine)**

Can you imagine what might have been going through the disciples' minds at this moment? They had only heard their Master speak this way one other time as recorded in John 6:51 where Jesus says, **"I am the living bread that came down from heaven. Anyone who eats this bread will live forever; this bread is my flesh, offered so the world may live."** The body of Jesus Christ was unlike that of any other human being.

In his gospel, Luke vividly portrays the birth of Christ. The angel Gabriel spoke to Mary the virgin chosen by God and said, **"The Holy Spirit will come upon you, and the power of the Most High will overshadow you; and for that reason the holy offspring shall be called the Son of God"**. Matthew quotes Isaiah by saying, **"Behold, the virgin shall be with child, and shall bear a son, and they shall call His name Immanuel, which translated means, 'God with us' "**. Then John in his gospel says, **"The Word became flesh"**.

If we take a further look at John's gospel, we will see that he goes from seeing Jesus as God taking upon Himself human flesh, to the words of John the Baptist who **"saw Jesus coming to him, and said, Behold, the Lamb of God who takes away the sin of the world (John 1:29)!"** John the Baptist, who was the prophet sent to prepare the way for the Messiah saw the true purpose of Christ, which was to be a pure sinless sacrifice, shedding His blood for all of humanity.

In John's first epistle he says, **"the Son of God appeared for this purpose, that He might destroy the works of the devil"** (I

John 3:8b). The only way that Satan could be defeated was through a man. It was the first man Adam, who had handed Satan his power and authority. Therefore, it had to be through a man, the Last Adam that Satan's power was to be destroyed. Hebrews 2:14-15 tells us that, **"because God's children are human beings – made of flesh and blood – Jesus also became flesh and blood by being born in human form. For only as a human being could he die, and only by dying could he break the power of the Devil, who had the power of death. Only in this way could he deliver those who have lived all their lives as slaves to the fear of dying."**

The Passover lamb to be sacrificed in Exodus 12:5, which was to be unblemished, merely pointed to the final sacrifice of Christ. The apostle Peter in his epistle calls Christ "**a lamb unblemished and spotless**" (I Peter 1:19b). On that night when Christ was partaking of that last Passover meal with His disciples, He was pointing them to His body, which was about to be beaten, crucified, and have the sin of the world lay upon it.

The *mystery of Christ* was about to be revealed. The scribes and Pharisees who were the interpreters of the prophets could not understand how the Messiah could be both a Conqueror and the Suffering Servant. However, the two main themes of the prophets came together in one person.

The *mystery of Christ* is that He broke the serpent's hold over man as a spotless, harmless, sinless lamb being slaughtered on the cross. When God became man in a human body, He was then offered up as a sheep being slaughtered and through His death on the cross the serpent's head was being crushed. Jesus handed the bread to His disciples and said eat this flesh. This flesh, which has no sin, is about to become sin for you!

WE MUST EAT AND DRINK

During the last Passover meal after Christ has pointed His disciples to His body, He now takes up the cup. Once He has drunk and given thanks, "He gave it to them saying, '**Drink from**

it, all of you; for this is My blood of the covenant, which is poured out for many for forgiveness of sins" (Matthew 26:28). As we look at this text we can see that the main theme of the New Covenant is the forgiveness of sins.

If I were to ask most Christians if their sins were forgiven, they would answer yes. However, we have to pause for a moment here and discover what it really means, to eat the flesh of Christ and drink in the 'blood of the covenant', so that we walk and live as a forgiven person. Drinking Christ blood is more than a prayer, but an active participation in the power of God by identifying totally with the crucified Lamb of God.

Untold numbers of people around the world have been made to believe that to be a Christian; all they have to do is say a prayer. For many, their Christian walk begins and ends at the altar. I grew up in a very large Evangelical denomination. One Sunday night at the age of 10 I went to the altar and made a confession of faith to accept Christ as my Savior.

Soon after my confession of faith, my family went through some very difficult times. My parents finally ended their marriage through a difficult divorce. To make a long story short, just as my parents went through a divorce, so I went through a divorce with my faith.

As I now look back upon this time in my life, my personal experience had much resemblance to the children of Israel in Egypt, who were the seed of Abraham, *yet they did not know God.* I was made to believe that just by saying a prayer and going to church, that I was a Christian. I know many who have made a confession of faith to Christ that are in the same position that I was in. They have said a prayer and some even go to church assembling with the children of God. However, they are in slavery to drugs, pornography, lying, adultery, fornication, legalism, etc., and do not even know or seek the heart of God.

I am not saying some of these people are not going to heaven, because only God knows that answer. In addition, we all have areas in our lives that God is working on. However, I am saying that there are many who have made a confession of faith, who are ignorant of their covenant responsibilities and rights as children of God. As long as we walk in ignorance we are being held in bondage to Satan and being kept from running in the race, which God has called us to.

I spent many years in ignorance, which resulted in my slavery to this worldly system and kept me out of the race. In the book of Exodus, we see that the very seed of Abraham who were promised to be the people through whom 'all the families of the earth' were going to be blessed, became the slaves of Egypt.

These were a people who were born with a destiny for greatness, just like you and I. However, because they were ignorant of their God given rights as the children of God they continued to settle for a life of bondage.

It was not until God gave Moses as a deliverer, that the children of Israel began to get a glimpse of the God of their inheritance. The children of Israel witnessed the awesome demonstration of the power of God as Moses and Aaron displayed signs and wonders before all of Egypt. However, it was only the Passover sacrifice that crushed the power of Pharaoh so that the children of Israel could be free from being the slaves of Egypt.

The Passover was a prophetic picture of the cross which crushed Satan's power over us, and which delivers us from slavery to the corruption of this present worldly system. It is in Exodus 12:7, after they sacrificed the lamb that the children of Israel were commanded to take the blood into a basin and then were told to put it on the post of the door. The applied blood to the door of the house was a covering. Wherever the blood was applied, the death angel would Passover and spare the firstborn.

> [9] "It would not have done Israel any good to know that there had to be the sacrifice of the Passover lamb or to have sacrificed it *unless they also applied its blood to their houses*. Likewise, it will not benefit us to just know that there had to be a propitiation for our sins – it will not even do us any good to know that Jesus made that propitiation – *unless His blood is applied to our life*. To just know facts without

applying them will accomplish nothing" (Emphasis Mine).

My problem was not that I did not know about the blood of the cross, but that I had never *applied the blood to my life*, nor *applied my life to the blood*; therefore, I was ignorant to the power it possessed.

There are many Christians who know what Christ has done for them, yet they have never applied their lives to the blood. One time I was ministering about this subject in Central Texas. In that part of the country, there are a lot of Pecan orchards. If you have ever eaten a pecan, and you're really good at cracking the shell, then you can open it up and what you will find is two sides to the nut inside, yet they are joined together at the bottom. It is one whole nut, yet there are two separate parts to it.

A whole pecan is a beautiful picture from nature to help us understand how to apply the blood covenant to our personal lives. On one side is what Christ has done for us on the cross. On the other side is our lives joined to and dedicated to the cross. *These two parts must be joined together, or it is not a covenant because a covenant involves two people.*

Jesus Christ has already fulfilled His side of the covenant, but until we become joined to what He has already done, we will never know the freedom of the cross. In Galatians 2:20 Paul the apostle explained to us how he applied the blood to his own life by saying, **"I have been crucified with Christ; and it is no longer I who live, but Christ lives in me."** Let's take a look at the gospel that Jesus taught and see what it truly means to 'eat His flesh and drink His blood'.

• IDENTIFICATION

On the same night that Jesus partook of the last Passover with His disciples, He was also taken into custody. Earlier during the evening, while they were still eating supper, Jesus told them that He would be taken into custody and that they would be scattered.

Peter, who usually spoke before he thought, said, "**Lord with You I am ready to go both to prison and to death!**" Yet, when it came down to having to really make that choice on that night, Peter chose to deny Christ, instead of paying a price by identifying with Him.

I know in retrospect we can all look at Peter and judge him for his lack of commitment, yet what would we have done? Do you know with the current trends going on in the world at least some sort of governmental persecution is looking like a possibility in the future even in the Western church?

The nation of England has had hate crimes legislation for about 10 years and it has affected the lives of Christians in that nation. In 2009 Dale Hurd a CBN reporter has documented the shift in England. He reported that in England [6] "Doctors, nurses, adoptive parents, are deemed unfit because of their Christian beliefs. Christians are told not to speak about God in the workplace or they could be punished for offending homosexuals or Muslims."

A similar form of 'hate crimes' legislation was instituted in the U.S. in 2009. I am not saying look out persecution is coming, but we are heading towards a slippery slope. At present the church in China not to mention Muslim nations, parts of India, and many other areas of the world are experiencing differing types of persecution. The history of the church is a history of resistance against true believers.

In the Greek language the word witness and martyr are the same word. This may seem radical to you, but it is simply part of the gospel. The biblical and historical record of the church is one of identifying with Christ in a hostile world.

What is happening in England seems to be moving to other Western nations. In the Western world persecution may not include physical torture, martyrdom or imprisonment as it did in Paul's day and for many believers in other parts of the world today. It is quite possible it will take the form of increasing marginalization as the mainstream of the surrounding culture moves in directions totally contradictory to the Bible that we cannot endorse. It could include discrimination against genuine Christians in nearly every aspect of life.

Right now in the world there are one hundred and ninety five political nations and in all but thirty true believers are facing some form of persecution. In the face of hate crimes legislation that number is greatly shrinking. We don't seek out nor do we want this reality, but we must understand how to face and live in a world, which is hostile to the kingdom of God. The only way to do this is to truly understand our identity in Christ and how that is lived out in a hostile world.

We are going to look through some scriptures in the Bible, to see what it really means to identify with Christ. We need to see what Jesus was really saying; when He told us we must eat His flesh and drink His blood.

To be identified with Christ, is surely more than just saying a prayer in an evangelistic meeting. This may be the first step in our identification with Him, but it is by far our last one. In John chapter 6, we can begin to peer into what it means to follow Christ. In John 6:53-56 Jesus says,

> "Truly, truly, I say to you, unless you eat the flesh of the Son of Man and drink His blood, you have no life in yourselves. He who eats My flesh and drinks My blood has eternal life, and I will raise him up on the last day. For My flesh is true food, and My blood is true drink. He who eats My flesh and drinks My blood abides in Me, and I in him."

In verse 52, the Jews had just asked Jesus how they could eat His flesh. Was he speaking of cannibalism? Of course Jesus was not talking about eating His physical flesh and blood, but He was speaking symbolically of a total identification with Him.

In Exodus 12:8, after Moses commanded the children of Israel to apply the blood to their door posts, he also told them to take the lamb, roast it with fire and to eat the flesh with unleavened bread and bitter herbs. Every Israelite who was delivered from Egypt not only had a blood covering, but they also had the lamb down inside of their stomachs. This lamb was eaten with unleavened bread and bitter herbs. The unleavened bread speaks of being separated from sin, and the bitter herbs speak of partaking of the sufferings, which come with being identified with Christ. When we truly partake of Christ and identify totally with Him, then we are going to begin to walk in liberty from the power of sin, yet we are also going to experience His sufferings.

You may say, "Well I want to walk in liberty from the power of sin, but I think I'll pass on experiencing His sufferings." Well my friend, you don't get to choose. There is no way to experience liberty from the power of sin without embracing the cross, and when you embrace the cross you will also embrace Christ's sufferings. This is what true discipleship is all about. When we identify with Christ we become dead to this world. As it is commonly said, the crucified thief could steal no more; the crucified murderer could no longer kill. The monkey that once jumped hard on your back has taken a fatal blow because he has been nailed to a tree. This is the freedom, which can be yours, if you will totally identify with Christ.

It is important at this point that I emphasize the grace of God. I am not speaking of a salvation based on works, but one that is solidly based on the grace of God. However, if we look at what the Bible teaches about the grace of God, many times it looks radically different than the way many people present the gospel of grace. Grace many times is presented as a license to sin and have God overlook it. Grace is not a license to sin, but the power of God manifested in Christ to strengthen us to not live under the slavery of sin.

Romans 6:1-2 "What shall we say then? Are we to continue in sin that *grace* might increase? May it never be! How shall we who died to sin still live in it?" (Emphasis mine)

Ephesians 2:8-9 "For by *grace* you have been saved through faith; and that not of yourselves, it is the gift of God; not as a result of works, that no one should boast." (Emphasis mine)

Titus 2:11-12 "For the *grace* of God has appeared, bringing salvation to all men, *instructing us to deny ungodliness and worldly desires and to live sensibly righteously and godly in the present age*"(Emphasis mine).

Grace is simply the gift of Christ. At the cross, Christ's grace was poured out so that we might be free from the power of sin. When we identify with Christ by partaking of His body and blood, then we will begin to grow in the grace of God. At the same time, to identify with Him will mean suffering with Him.

Romans 8:18 "For I consider that the sufferings of this present age are not worthy to be compared with the glory that is to be revealed to us."

I Peter 4:1 "Therefore, since Christ has suffered in the flesh, arm yourselves also with the same purpose, because he who has suffered in the flesh has ceased from sin."

II Corinthians 12:9 "My grace is sufficient for you, for My power is perfected in weakness." Most gladly, therefore, I will rather boast about my weaknesses, that the power of Christ may dwell in me."

This last scripture reference has been greatly debated as to what Paul was actually speaking about in regards to his weaknesses. I believe if we take everything into context and do not read our own interpretations into this section of scripture, then II Corinthians 12:10 becomes the thorn in the flesh and the weaknesses that Paul was referring to. Our cross is not sickness and disease, but it will mean facing insults, distresses, persecution and difficulties in life. This is no way saying that you may not experience sickness and disease, but it is not our loving Father's hand bringing it to your life. Jesus said we would face tribulation in this world, but when He walks with us, we will overcome just as He overcame.

No matter how we interpret II Corinthians 12:9 we cannot get around the fact that we are going to experience suffering by identifying with Christ. I'll use an analogy in the natural and ask if you have ever run a mile without experiencing some suffering? What about a marathon? As you run this race with Christ you will discover what it means to suffer with Him, but at the same time you will discover the power of the grace of God, which will develop in your heart as you learn to dwell in Him and He in you.

● FELLOWSHIP

At the same time that we are identifying with Christ by partaking of His body and blood, we are also entering into a fellowship with Him and all of those who have identified with Him.

When we look at fellowship, what we begin to peer into is what the Bible calls the 'mystery of Christ'. Paul unfolds this mystery in the book of Colossians by saying that this mystery **"is Christ in you"** (Colossians 1:27).

Paul goes on to say that his sole purpose in ministry was to present every man complete in Christ. Following Christ and becoming more like Him is the essence of Christianity. It is for this purpose that we have been saved and it is through fellowship with Him and one another that this is achieved.

On that last Passover night when Jesus was laying down the very foundations of the New Covenant, He laid that foundation down on the bedrock of fellowship. We see in Paul the apostle's letter to the Corinthian Church that he has to bring them back to this foundation of fellowship. In speaking to the Corinthians Paul says:

> "For I have received from the Lord that which I also delivered to you, that the Lord Jesus in the night in which He was betrayed took bread; and when He had given thanks, He broke it and said, 'This is my body, which is broken for you; do this in remembrance of Me.' In the same way He took the

cup also, after supper, saying, 'This cup is the new covenant in My blood; do this, as often as you drink it, in remembrance of Me.'" (I Corinthians 23-25)

In chapter 10 Paul was just speaking to the wise men of Corinth and asking them, "**Is not the cup of blessing which we bless a** SHARING **in the blood of Christ?   Is not the bread which we break a** SHARING **in the body of Christ?" (Emphasis Mine)**

It is through the Greek word used for sharing, that we have developed the English word for communion. Today when we hear the word communion, we think of a church service, where at the end we eat bread and drink grape juice (or wine depending on your theology) together, celebrating the death, resurrection, and return of Christ. We should practice this as a body and experience its life giving power.

> [11] "The breaking of bread reminds us of the cross upon which our Lord's Body was Broken. Bread is made from the crushed wheat. Wine is made from the pressed gape. Both elements represent death.
>
> The breaking of bread not only depicts the death of Christ, it also shows forth His resurrection. The grain of wheat has gone into the ground. Yet it now lives to produce many grains like itself (John 12:24). Thus if we eat Christ's flesh and drink His Blood, we obtain His life (John 6:53). This is resurrection – life out of death."

However, there is more to communion than the ceremony we observe together.

Communion is an English translation of the Greek word *Koinōnia* that is defined as: "Fellowship with, participation in anything, the using of a thing in common." The word *Koinōnia* is the word that I believe best demonstrates how we apply the work of the cross to our lives. Let's take a quick look at this word, which can be translated as sharing, fellowship and communion.

What is demonstrated through the Greek word *Koinōnia* is simply an unveiling of the 'mystery of Christ', which is Christ living in and through the life of the believer.

When I think of the word *Koinōnia,* I think of the word partnership. We are in a partnership with Christ and His body the church. In Matthew 11:29, Jesus instructs us to come to Him and take upon ourselves His yoke. To be yoked to Christ is to become His partner. A partner shares, loves and works together. The essence of the New Covenant is that through Christ's redeeming work on the cross, man can now be brought into a partnership with God.

It is no longer to be us living life through our own ability, but Christ living in and through us. Religion is man trying to be a Christian. No man has ever been able to live the Christian life except for Christ Himself! This is why Paul said, it is no longer I who live, but Christ lives in me. Through the Spirit of Christ we become 'partakers' of the divine nature (II Peter 1:4).

When we become partakers of the divine nature through the new birth experience, then we are also partaking of the Spirit of resurrection life. When Christ is living in us and we are identifying with Him, then we are His body in this earth.

NEW BEGINNINGS

When we truly lay down our lives at the cross, we experience a death to ourselves, yet we also experience the new life that comes from being raised up with Christ.

It is interesting to look at Exodus 12:1-2. When Moses prepared Israel for the first Passover, he was instructed to rotate the calendar and make it the first month of the year. When Jesus partook of that last Passover meal with His disciples, He emphasized this same truth by declaring His own body and blood to be the opening of a New Covenant. However, the change that we partake of is not a physical change of time or location, but a spiritual transformation of the heart.

When we identify with Christ as our Passover lamb, we are born again and by the power of the Spirit we enter into the kingdom of God. We undergo an inward spiritual change unlike that of Israel who experienced a change in physical location.

The main scriptural passage that we use for understanding the new birth is in John 3:1-8. The new birth is the power of the Holy Spirit at work, totally transforming a soul's eternal destiny. It is not some religious ceremony based on our own works, which is the equivalent of putting a Band-Aid on to straighten a broken leg. Jesus didn't tell Nicodemus he needed a new religious program, but that he actually needed to go through a new birth. The world mocks us when we talk about being born again, but it is the foolishness of the cross that creates a new heart.

In the last chapter I clearly showed you that the 'unspiritual nature' is good for nothing but the cross. Jesus told Nicodemus, one of the most highly respected religious men of his day, that he must be 'born from above'. Natural birth gets us into this world of the flesh, but it is only through spiritual new birth that we enter into the spiritual life of the kingdom of God. This is not something that you can do on your own. Only God can perform this supernatural act in your heart. The new birth is being born of God through His Spirit, as you lay your wicked heart of stone at the cross and He gives you a new heart.

This new heart that the Spirit of God has put within you has been made to respond to your new head. In understanding the new birth, we need to understand that Christ takes over the headship of our lives. We love to hear how our sins have been forgiven, and about all of the promises that become ours in Christ, but many refuse to completely surrender their hearts to Jesus as Lord over their entire lives.

If you want to begin the race on the right foot, then you must come to realize that "**your body is a temple of the Holy Spirit who is in you, whom you have from God, and that you are not your own**" (I Corinthians 6:19). You don't get to run the way that you want to, but you must learn the yoke of Christ, for that is the only pathway to true success. Biblical success is following Christ and completing His will for our lives.

OUR POINT OF REFERENCE FOR RUNNING

The cross should be more than just an historical picture in our minds; we should continually be partaking of the 'body and blood' of Christ. To keep the cross as our point of reference does not mean that we don't learn anything else in the Bible. However, it does mean that the understanding of the cross and the foundational doctrines of Christ have been laid down solidly within our hearts and that this foundation is what keeps us on the right track.

Once we have laid a strong foundation and have a solid understanding of the other basic truths of the faith that are listed in Hebrews 6:1-2, we must learn how to use what we have been given (To further study Hebrews 6:1-2 go to www.FoundationPub.org to get a free copy of "Building Your Spiritual House" or Like our Facebook Fan Page at FoundationMin.) The reason you take driving lessons is so you can learn how to drive. What is the use of taking lessons, if you are not going to use what you have learned? Maturity is learning how to put into practice what you have learned.

It is a wonderful thing to be born again, but being born is just the beginning of life. We must go on to maturity. We must set our vision on the calling for which we have been made a new creation.

The cross is simply our foundation or our point of reference that keeps us going in the right direction. Being a disciple of the Lord Jesus Christ is the process of learning how to allow Christ to live His life through us. Each person has a calling and Christ in each person will fulfill a distinct function and purpose.

CHAPTER 4

VISION: THE MOTIVATION TO RUN

"Where there is no vision the people are unrestrained."
Proverbs 29:18

What is it that has caused men and women of faith to run their race in the face trials, temptations, persecutions and difficulties without giving up? (Hebrews 11:35-38) One word can describe such people, committed! Anyone who has ever accomplished a great task for Christ was more than just a casual follower of Him. A disciple's life is one, which will be marked by a continued persistence to complete the will of God, by fulfilling the vision which God has entrusted to them.

Why is it that a lone monk by the name of Martin Luther had the courage to stand up against the religious leaders of his day? This one man's ideas challenged the entire religious system of his time and because of this he eventually lost his reputation for speaking out against the corruption of the church during the Middle Ages? Yet, through this one man's vision an entire movement, which changed the face of the earth, was born.

500 years later Martin Luther King Jr. a black Baptist preacher in the south had the strength to endure beatings, jailing, slander, financial loss and the list of injustices goes on! All the odds were against him. However, as he surrendered to God's vision for his life he impacted American society for great change. Although he was killed by an assassin's bullet even today he inspires others to 'Dream his dream'.

It was during the reign of the Persian Empire, God placed a young Jewish woman named Esther in a place of great influence. Through her courage and willingness to risk her life, the entire Jewish race was rescued. What gave her the courage to risk everything? It was only as she was awakened to the fact that she was born for that particular time. As she laid hold of the vision for which God had ordained for her, she was moved to greatness and even today her life is remembered through the Jewish Celebration of Purim.

The list could go on of godly businessmen and women who pursued their dreams by tapping into God's wisdom for the fulfilling of their purpose. I could list actors, writers, scientist, educators and yes even politicians who have lived their lives by the vision of Christ for their lives impacting this world for the kingdom of God.

I believe besides Christ, we have no greater pattern to follow than Paul the apostle. In writing his own biography Paul says, **"Five times I received from the Jews forty lashes minus one, three times I was beaten with rods, once I was stoned three times I was shipwrecked, for a night and a day I have been adrift at sea."** (II Corinthians 11:24-26) Paul goes on to continue his list of difficulties he encountered running his race. What kept these people of faith running, as they encountered one difficulty after another to keep them from fulfilling their calling in life?

Paul gives away the secret behind his motivation when speaking to King Agrippa. He tells the king that he was not **"disobedient to the HEAVENLY VISION."** (Acts 26:19) (Emphasis Mine) As all other great men and women of faith who have ever accomplished anything of lasting value, they were people captivated and governed by vision.

Paul was a person who was motivated to fulfill a vision that God had entrusted to Him. Paul was totally convinced of God's calling on his life and constantly worked towards the fulfillment of God's purpose. It was a God inspired vision, which motivated Paul to commit his life to working out that vision in his daily life.

Two-tiered Vision of Christ

It is important before we go on from here, to understand   what I can best describe as a two-tiered vision of Christ. God is always working through this two-tiered vision. The FIRST-TIER is **God's eternal purposes accomplished through Christ.** This is the foundation and starting point of all vision. The SECOND-TIER is **God's eternal purposes accomplished through each member of His body upon the earth, the church.**

Paul the apostle unfolds this two-tiered vision in the book of Ephesians. In Ephesians 1:4-5 he tells us that, **"Long ago, even before he made the world, God loved us and chose us in Christ to be holy and without fault in his eyes.   His unchanging plan has always been to adopt us into his own family by bringing us to himself through Jesus Christ and this gave him great pleasure."** (New Living Translation) There is no higher calling than sonship! God restoring His glory to humanity is His highest priority. Every man, woman and child coming under the headship of Christ is God's ultimate purpose (Ephesians 1:10).

God has a vision of each member of His body being conformed to the image of His Son (Romans 8:29). The essence of Paul's apostolic prayer in Ephesians 1:17-23, contains the pattern for accomplishing our ultimate destiny, which is Christ-likeness. The first ingredient for accomplishing this goal is a prayer for spiritual vision.

Paul's prayer for these believers or disciples in Ephesus was that they would be given **"a spirit of wisdom and of revelation in the knowledge of Him** (Christ)." He then prayed that the eyes of their hearts would be open to know:

1) The hope of **His calling**.

2) The riches of the glory of **His inheritance in them**.

3) The surpassing greatness of **His power toward them**.

Let's break this prayer down because I believe in this prayer, we will see what motivated Paul. Paul told Agrippa that he was motivated to fulfill God's **'HEAVENLY VISION'** for his life. He was praying that these disciples would become heavenly minded.

I have heard it said that many Christians are so **"heavenly minded that they are no earthly good."** A friend of mine says that many Christians are so **"earthly minded they are no heavenly good!"** Yes, heavenly vision with no practical outlet is simply mysticism. However, to have an eternal impact upon this planet, we must have the eyes of our hearts opened so that we can live this life from a heavenly perspective. It is only by living from God's heavenly vision, that we will be motivated to accomplish His purposes on this earth for our daily lives.

The first thing Paul prayed for was a spirit of wisdom and of revelation in the knowledge of Christ. Paul was praying for more than a mere 'head knowledge'. The problem we have today is that many Christians have 'head knowledge' of Christ, yet their lives are not changed. They have not committed their lives to the cross. They acknowledge the importance of the cross, yet they still live by the 'lower nature'. Their hearts have not been captured by the 'word of the cross'. Yes, they will tell you they are Christians, yet you can tell by their lifestyles that their lives still belong to themselves. They have retained lordship over their own hearts and Christ has little or no place in their lives. This is why sin has a hold upon them and is many times totally unrestrained in their lives! Proverbs 29:18 tells us that where there is no vision then people live unrestrained lives. Vision harnesses us to God's purpose and restrains our conduct to come into alignment with the intended will of God.

The word Paul uses for knowledge in Ephesians 1:17 is the Greek word *Epignōsis*. This word goes beyond superficial shallow head knowledge of something. It expresses a *thorough participation* in the object of knowledge. "In the New Testament this word appears only in the Pauline writings and in Heb. 10:26, II Peter 1:2,3,8; 2:20, and always refers to knowledge which very powerfully influences the form of the spiritual life, a knowledge laying claim to personal sympathy and exerting an influence upon the person." (Lexical Aids to the New Testament) Paul was praying that their hearts would be radically touched through the wisdom and revelation of the crucified and risen Christ. He prayed that their lives would become an expression of the life of Christ.

We must have a true vision of Christ communicated to our hearts. It is only by seeing and relating with Him, that we can fulfill our purpose. As we see Him clearly then and only then will we no longer grope around in this dark world living a life of unrestrained sin. When our hearts are opened to Him, we will become identified with Him and will experience daily spiritual growth to become more like Him.

So many people are running around wanting their vision to be fulfilled, yet it is only by first aligning our hearts to His vision that we will ever find our true purpose. All true vision is lived out of a reference point of the foundation of a vision of Christ.

Paul prayed that the eyes of our hearts would be opened, so that we could become intimately connected to His calling. If you want to know your calling then become acquainted with **HIS CALLING**. He then prayed that we would understand **HIS INHERITANCE IN US** (Lordship) and finally that we would experience **HIS POWER TOWARD US** for the accomplishing of His vision.

Christ is working out His dominion and rule over Satan through us, His inheritance. God wants to manifest the wisdom and power of the cross through His church. Ephesians 3:11 says that this is in **"accordance with the eternal purpose which He carried out through Christ Jesus our Lord."**

No matter what specific vision or calling God has placed upon your life, you have been commissioned to fulfill the 'Great Commission.' (Matthew 28) We have been called to proclaim Christ's victory over darkness. He has called every disciple to preach the gospel. He has given you authority over darkness to set the oppressed free.

I remember when I was only 21 years old. The church I was working with asked me to go down and pick up this street person at the Mc Donald's in town and take him to a shelter. I went down there and put him in my car but he refused to go to a shelter. I ended up taking him home with me. I was getting him something to eat while he was sitting on my couch. Before I finished, I had a leading to pray for him. I laid my hands on his head and began to pray, when I simply spoke the name of Jesus. This man started going into convulsions and spit up white foam from his mouth. I did not even realize the full extent of what was happening, but I cast an evil spirit out of this man.

Each member of Christ's body has been anointed to preach the gospel with power. We have not only been called to be more like Jesus, but also, to do the works, which He did. It is going to take people walking in their place under His leadership to help fulfill the Great Commission.

This brings us to the SECOND-TIER of vision, which is God's eternal purposes, accomplished through each individual member of His body. We each have a common foundation, but we also each have an individual part to fulfill, which makes us unique in God's mighty plan. The Holy Spirit empowers us to be like Christ and also to be ourselves. This is called the manifold wisdom of God (Ephesians 3:10). Just as Joseph had a coat of many colors, so God has woven a beautiful tapestry together called the body of Christ. The body is made up of many individual colors masterfully woven together through the wisdom of God to display the likeness of Christ.

Christ wants each member of His body to come under His headship so that they can receive His vision for their lives. God has a ministry specifically hand tailored to fit your unique personality. He has gifted each part of His body to bring forth an expression of Himself. It is important in these days that members catch a glimpse of the vision that God wants them to walk in. It is His vision for us that will give us the wisdom and power to live a disciplined life with purpose and direction. The Christian leader George Barna in his book "The Power of Vision" says:

> [12] "Unless God's people have a clear vision of where they are headed, the probability of a successful journey is severely limited. Unless you attend to His call upon your life and ministry, you are likely to

experience confusion, weariness, dissipation and impotence.

You can see the importance of vision for ministry in the lives of virtually every significant Christian leader, ranging from such ancient leaders as Abraham to such modern leaders as Billy Graham."

Any man or woman who has ever accomplished anything of significance has been a person of vision. True vision comes down from above. It comes as we pray the prayer Christ told us to pray. "Thy kingdom come on earth as it is in heaven." As disciples we are called to seek first the kingdom, then we will have imparted by the Holy Spirit, His **wisdom** to know the mind of God and His **power** to fulfill His kingdom purposes. Godly vision is a gift coming down from the Father above. It is not conjured or worked up, but it comes when we learn to align our hearts to the outflowing of His abundance of grace.

THE MANIFOLD GRACE OF GOD

Yes, many people talk about grace these days, but we need realize all that grace implies. Peter uses the term **manifold grace of God** in his epistle (I Peter 4:10) and I believe this will help us to get a broader foundation of the fullness of grace. The word *manifold* simply means *varied*. That means there is more than just one aspect of grace.

I want to briefly describe what I call three levels of grace.

1) Grace **working for you.**

2) Grace **working in you.**

3) Grace **working through you.**

As I have already said in chapter 3 of this book that grace defined to its simplest form is the free gift of Christ. Now we will look to the book of Romans to help us understand grace. The book of Romans has been called the gospel of God's grace. It is in Romans 3:24, where we see that from the cross flows grace. It declares that we have been made right with God **"as a gift by His grace through the redemption (the cross) which is in Christ Jesus."** This was not because we were good, but because God's love was poured out upon us and we simply responded. As a result of our response, faith was activated in our hearts, and we were set free from Satan's power over our lives. This erased the guilt of sin. This was God's grace working on our behalf. Grace is GOD'S POWER WORKING FOR US.

However, grace does not stop at just setting us free from the guilt of sin. Grace continues to work in us, setting us free from sin's power, so that Christ can fill our lives with His goodness. In Romans, chapters 6 through 8, Paul describes the power of grace working in us by the ministry of the Holy Spirit. Grace working in us gives us a vision of growing up into the full stature of Christ.

One thing you must understand. Grace is not an excuse for sin. *Grace is the power to live a life free from sin!* Read Romans 6 through 8 for yourself. Yes, Romans chapter 7 shows us that there will be a struggle in dealing with the 'lower nature', yet it is not an excuse to live a life dominated by sin. The only reason anyone is living a life dominated by sin, is because they don't have a clear vision of Christ. The Spirit of Grace is GODS POWER WORKING IN YOU, which gives you a sanctified life. Sanctification simply means you have been set apart for the purpose of God through 'GRACE WORKING IN YOU'.

It is in Romans chapter 12 where we see Paul begin to define what I call 'GRACE WORKING THROUGH YOU'. Paul tells each of us to not think more of ourselves than we should, **"but to think so as to have sound judgment, as God has allotted to each a measure of faith. For just as we have many members in one body and ALL THE MEMBERS DO NOT HAVE THE SAME FUNCTION, so we, who are many, are one body in Christ, and individually members one of another. And since we have**

GIFTS THAT DIFFER ACCORDING TO THE GRACE GIVEN TO US, LET EACH EXERCISE THEM accordingly" (Emphasis Mine). We could also call this the outworking of grace or 'heavenly vision' being lived out practically in our lives.

As I begin to use these scriptures along with some others, I hope to remove a common lie, one that has made its way into the church. This lie says, "I can be and do anything I set my mind to." No you cannot! This is a satanic lie meant to take you beyond God given vision. According to the Bible you can only be and do that which God has graced you to be and do. In speaking about election and calling, Paul says, "it does not depend on the man who wills or the man who runs, but on God..." (Romans 9:16) It is God who has made you. Do you the clay; tell the potter how you want to be made? No you just put yourself into the potter's hands and let Him mold you, into the vessel that He wants you to be. This is what it means, when Paul tells us not to think more highly of ourselves than we ought to think. He is saying that we must humble ourselves, under the grace that has been given to us.

Did Paul make himself an apostle? No! Again and again he opens his writings by saying Paul "called as an apostle" or "Paul, an apostle of Christ Jesus according to the will of God." It is not what Paul chose, he just learned how to yield himself to the grace given to him. He says "by the grace of God I am what I am, and His grace toward me did not prove vain; but I labored even more than all of them, yet not I, but the grace of God with me." (I Corinthians 15:10) That is grace in action working through us to fulfill the vision of God for our lives.

I have met my share of what I call 'want to be prophets'. That is all they are. They may have given a simply prophecy here or there and have some spiritual insight but have not been given the grace to be a prophet (Read "The Established Foundation" appendix A, B and C for a further explanation on the difference between prophets, prophecy and the manifestation of the Spirit of prophecy in the church.) Yet, they are staking their entire lives and future on being a prophet. There are too many of those who 'want to be'. People who tend to think more highly of themselves than they should and have based their futures on an inflated opinion of themselves. It is time we accurately assess the grace that has been given to us. If you have been graced to run a business, don't try and be an apostle. You may be equipped by that gift to do certain apostolic functions, but that does not make you an apostle.

God never gives us vision for something He has not graced our lives to accomplish. Each person has been given a certain gifting. We need to identify that which God has given to us and learn how to completely yield our lives to that which is the will of God for our lives. Our God given gifts will help explain why we do things the way we do.

In the same place where it talks about the manifold grace of God in I Peter 4:10 the apostle also says that, "**each of you has received a gift.**" In the Amplified version of the Bible, this verse becomes very clear. "**As each of you have received a gift (a particular spiritual talent, a gracious divine endowment), employ it for one another as [befits] good trustees of God's many-sided grace – faithful stewards of the extremely diverse [powers and gifts granted to Christians by] unmerited favor. Whoever SPEAKS, [let him do it as one who utters] oracles of God; whoever RENDERS SERVICE, [let him do it] as with the strength which God furnishes abundantly..."**

In Romans 12, where it lists the differing gifts of grace given to each member of the body, you will see that some gifts are used by *SPEAKING* such as prophecy, teaching, exhortation and some gifts are used by *SERVING* such as service, giving, leading and mercy. One is not more important than the other, but each has their place and purpose. We need you to be you. You cannot be someone else, but you can be the best you there could ever be.

We are simply a part and not the whole. As a member of Christ's body we have been given a grace to function as an effective part of His body. Therefore, let us rise up and exercise the grace given to us.

MEASURE OF RULE

God's vision for our lives is always exercised in what I call our 'measure of rule'. Paul, whom I could safely call the most effective apostle in the New Testament times, realized that he was not called to do everything. He could not be everywhere or change the whole world by himself. Although we each have a specific calling and vision it is limited to the 'measure of rule' God has distributed to us.

Nobody has been called to reach the whole world! You may have a ministry, which will help mobilize others, but your vision for reaching the entire world is just an arrogant dream conjured up through an inflated ego. Even large ministries and businesses have a 'measure of rule' for their ministries and products. It may be a large measure, due to faithfulness over the years, yet they are limited to just being a part not the all in all. Teachers are best when they stay in their realm of expertise. If you are a good accountant then don't try and be a marketing director but stay within the measure of rule your gift gives you. Yes, the body of Christ is being mobilized to preach the gospel to all nations, however *it is going to take the entire body to accomplish this task and you are just a part of the whole.*

Paul in speaking of his apostolic ministry says, **"We shall not boast extravagantly but rather stay within the limit of the sphere which God has allotted to us."** (II Corinthians 10:13 New Berkley Version) Paul understood that he was not called to do everything, nor go everywhere, but that God had given him a specific vision for ministry and specific places to impact.

In looking at our 'measure of rule', we need to see it in regards to both our VISIONARY CALLING along with its BOUNDARIES. This can be clearly seen in Paul the apostle's life. Paul tells us that his distinct visionary calling was to minister to the Gentiles. In Acts 28, when Paul was speaking of his 'heavenly vision', he says that Jesus specifically told him, that he was being sent to preach to the Gentiles. This is further clarified in Galatians 2:7-9, when Paul is referring to his visit with the elders of the church in Jerusalem.

Paul in referring to his visit with these elders says, **"seeing that I had been entrusted with the gospel to the uncircumcised (Gentiles), just as Peter had been to the circumcised (Jews)**

(for He who effectually worked for Peter in his apostleship to the circumcised effectually worked for me also to the Gentiles), and RECOGNIZING THE GRACE THAT HAD BEEN GIVEN TO ME....gave to me and Barnabas the right hand of fellowship that we might go to the Gentiles, and they to the circumcised (Jews)." (Emphasis Mine) Paul was defining his calling and restricting it, to that which God had called him to do.

In looking at Paul as a sent one, it is important that we understand, he only went where the Holy Spirit would allow him to go. It is God's desire to restore this apostolic understanding to the church. We not only need to know what the Lord has sent us to accomplish, but we also need to know where He wants us to accomplish His work. (Acts 16:6-10)

Since God has limited us to a certain 'measure of rule' in our vision and calling, we must learn how to flow with others. This makes team work an utter necessity.

TEAM WORK

God has so composed His body, that it demands teamwork. Biblically speaking, *teamwork is not an option, but the only way for effective vision to be implemented and accomplished.* If you look at any successful church, business, ministry, community or family; a common ingredient is 'team work'.

In looking at biblical examples, it is easy to see that God has always worked through teams: Moses and Aaron, Joshua and Caleb, Jesus and his apostles, Paul, Barnabas, Silas, Timothy and Titus. In addition, we have the husband and wife team of Aquilla and Priscilla. The list could go on. Jesus gathered a core team together who were joined to Him, and to one another. In fact this was one of His highest priorities. This also became a priority with His sent apostles and it is still a priority. He desires us to have a vision to work as a team member.

God never has and never will give just one person everything. Yes, a team will have a leader, but even the leader is just a part. A visionary leader will give direction and guidance. However, the leader's task is to help each team member reach their full potential and cause the team to accomplish their God given task.

In life, you soon realize that you cannot run with everyone. You will not see eye to eye or be able to be on a team with just anyone. You are a specific part of the body and you are not called to work side by side with every part. A toe is part of your body in the same way that your eye is, but they do not function in close proximity to one another. Yes, the Bible commands us to love all, but that does not mean we will be able to be a team member with everyone. There are core people that God has specifically tailored for you to labor in the kingdom of God beside.

At the same time, there are seasons in everyone's life. Just as a football player may play with Tampa Bay for five years, then be traded to Pittsburgh, so it is in the church. You may serve with one team (church or ministry) for a season, then God will re-align the team and put you in a different position or on another team (church or ministry) altogether. Look at Paul and Barnabas in the book of Acts. They worked as a team for years then Paul took Timothy and Barnabas took Mark. There are some who see this as division, but I see it as multiplication. God knows where we are needed and where we will be the most productive, as we are running this race in each season of our lives.

Ephesians 4:11-16 teaches us about teamwork. In vs. 11 Paul begins by talking about the gifts of the Resurrected Christ, given for the equipping of the saints. Christ in His wisdom for the building of the church has distributed His anointing to a plurality of leaders who have a diversity of gifting. Each has been given an aspect of Christ. No man or woman has been given everything. This is so we will learn how to work as a team.

As we go through these verses, we will see that it is God's desire for us to mature, be in unity, become stable in our faith and learn to work together. In vs. 16, he says that as a body we are to be fitted **"and held together by that which every joint supplies, according to the proper working of each individual part."** A joint is not a part, but it is where two parts come together. God wants to fit us rightly together with others for the fulfilling of His purpose in our lives.

A term that has become popular in the business world is synergy. *Synergy is the working together of two things to produce an effect greater than the sum of the parts.* The emphasis is no longer on hostile takeovers but on corporations merging in order to take advantage of 'common synergies'. Rather than swallowing direct competitors, companies are diversifying their range of expertise by merging or purchasing a company with complementary strengths.

Synergistic leadership is about fellowship, participation and community. It is about learning to combine our efforts together for the common good and a common goal. However, to be able to work together on a team, we must have a common vision and a common faith. Amos 3:3 asks the question, **"Can two walk together, except they be in agreement?"** (King James Version) It will be of necessity that you are able to humble yourself and come into agreement with others. You must not think more highly or lowly of yourselves, but humble yourselves and join hands with others in running your race.

RUNNING IN DIVINE ORDER

In the book of Hebrews, which goes into great detail about Jesus Christ being a King-Priest after the order of Melchizedek, it tells us to come boldly to the throne of grace. A throne denotes approaching a king. We are to approach our King on the basis of grace, yet there is also a divine order of government in every kingdom. True vision never breaks the governmental order of the kingdom of God.

When looking at teamwork, we also need to understand that with every team there must also be order. An abundance of leadership theories exist and differing ones may be more appropriate depending on the purpose being accomplished. In this book I am simply talking about the most basic things needed to fulfill your vision.

A team without order is a team without direction and discipline. A team leader is always a visionary. Whether it is a family, church, business, ministry or community, there is a leader or group of leaders who set the order and the pace of the race.

A common scenario for many people when they begin to receive vision from God is to think they are the only ones with vision. Yet, if that is your attitude, it is a sure sign that you are immature in your vision.

Children are self-centered and only think of themselves. They must be trained to incorporate their gifts for the greater whole. I John 2:12 shows us three levels of growth that we go through. That is children, young men and fathers. When we are children we will be dependent and focused upon meeting our needs, our wants and our way. As we grow into young adults, then we take a more independent outlook on things. This is not necessarily bad, but a natural part of growth. The last stage of growth is fathers and this is where we learn to take our vision and cause it to be interdependent with others.

If you have received a vision from God for a particular calling then get around some mature team leaders who can train you and cause you to grow into your ultimate vision. Walk along side them with a humble heart to learn. Be willing to lay down your life and serve.

If you will be faithful in helping someone else, it will help you discover if you are a visionary leader or someone whose calling is to support and help in the greater vision of a church, business or non-profit organization. If you are a visionary leader then your faithfulness will pay off. The Bible says if you will be faithful over that which is another man's then God will give you your own. It really can be a win-win situation for everyone involved if the motives remain pure.

In a day when every man does what is right in his own eyes, we need to come under the divine order of the kingdom of God. There is a divine order for your life and vision.

If you are single then the kingdom of God sets an order for your life. Paul told us that single people should be singularly focused upon the things of God. Single people you need to take advantage of your time. Stop searching after a mate and start searching after the heart and will of God for your lives. I was saved at the age of 19 and did not marry until the age of 26. I am very grateful for the years I spent as a single Christian. There are many things a single Christian can do, which is more difficult and sometimes impossible for a married Christian to accomplish. God wants to use single people in these last days. It is easier for singles to travel, live and provide for themselves. Don't let the disorder of pre-marital sex and pleasure keep you from the purpose of God. Seek first His kingdom and become a willing participant in His will for your life. God will provide for you at the right time the godly mate you will need for the fulfilling of His purpose.

Every vision is simply a part of the larger purposes of Christ for His church. For example, a husband and wife must have unity in their relationship. It is only when unity is maintained, that God's vision can be fulfilled. A husband and a wife are a team. They do not receive a vision from God then independently carry it out. God is not the author of confusion, nor of rebellion, rather He is the God of order. I have witnessed more than one Christian couple paralyzed in vision, because they failed to walk in unity together.

God has not only established order in our personal lives, but also in His church. You may be one of those people who have been hurt through church relationships. As long as you let past hurts paralyze you it will be impossible to fulfill your God given vision. Even if the church has hurt you or its leadership the reality is that God has ordained His church to be the vehicle of the kingdom. Men and women of God are not perfect, yet God uses these earthen vessels for His kingdom purposes. Find the team with which you can work.

You may say, I can't find a church where I can be a team player. You must pray, pursue and be willing to change your heart so you can fit where it pleases God. It is possible you may even need to change geographical locations. Find a church where you can be a useful part.

In defining the church I am not saying that you have to follow any particular pattern. Millions of believers in the U.S. and worldwide are redefining what the church is or you might say they are looking to the New Testament and discovering that the church is not a building, but a people. The Father has a family of people for you to work together in fulfilling His purpose for your life. It is usually when we are thinking more highly of ourselves than we should that we have a hard time fitting. Appraise yourself honestly, so that you can cooperate with others in running your race. At the same time, don't put on Saul's armor just to be accepted, because you will not be able to run effectively. You can only be yourself and when others expect you to conform to their image; you have departed from the grace of God. God has a place for you! You can't run alone you need a team.

We need to learn to recognize order and authority anywhere we go. There is order and authority in any church, business, home, city or country into which you may go. Recognizing this will help you not trip, while you are running, but will teach you to work as a team player wherever you go.

RUNNING BY THE POWER OF YOUR WORDS

The amazing thing about living a life from vision is that it is really living the God-kind of life. The first thing that we discover about God's nature in the Bible is His creative nature.

God is the Creator and when He created the heavens, earth and all that is therein, He created man. Man was created in God's image and according to His likeness (Genesis 1:26).

> [13] "The Hebrew word translated into the English word likeness means 'to operate like,' not 'to look like.' God's original design for man requires that we function like God."

God has put within every man his creative power. We have been made to function as a creator in life. Life's circumstances are not to be the directing force of our life, but the creative power and wisdom of God's vision is to be the motivating source of our decisions and direction.

We are simply earthen vessels made from the dust of the earth. Since this is true, it is imperative that as new creations, we learn to yield these clay jars (our bodies), to the surpassing glory of Christ's resurrection power and His descending wisdom.

On a practical level, the creative power and wisdom of vision can only be released, as we learn to write down our vision and speak it out. The prophet Habakkuk was told to write down God's vision, so that those who read it would be able to run (Habakkuk 2:1-3).

Vision gives us focus, purpose and the motivation to run. Vision removes the darkness and debris from our minds so we can see the path we are running on clearly. It is only through vision that people can truly be joined together as a team. I hope that you go to a church, work for a business or live in a home where the vision has been written down and articulated. For you to fulfill your part you have to know why the team exists, where it is going and what the team wishes to accomplish.

Writing and speaking vision gives us guidance and strength to run. On a practical, level this is the principle of setting goals. What kinds of goals do you have? What are you running towards for the ultimate fulfillment of your vision? Answer that question for me, and I can tell you how much purpose and motivation you have in your life.

The author William H. Cook says that, "goal-setting for the Christian is simply planned, organized, stretching under the lordship of Christ." Having a goal or vision is more than just a good idea, but a God-inspired idea. We must take God's inspired ideas; write them down, plan, pray, organize and then speak them over our lives so that they direct our paths. If we want our goals to be truly motivating, they must become specific. The more clearly defined the goal the more likely it is we will be able to fulfill it and others will be able follow.

[14]"Having a goal that is too general may be worse than not having one at all. General goals are seldom attained and lead only to frustration. Those who 'want to get rich', or 'go into business for themselves,' seldom do."

It is important that we set both short and long-term goals. If we want to be successful, we must go beyond just being dreamers. Goals help us to set marks by which we can allow the plans of God to take root in our lives.

One of your long-term goals may be to become just like Jesus, which is God's ultimate vision for each of our lives (Romans 8:29). What are you doing today to accomplish that task? Are you beholding His face through prayer, worship and the study of His word? When He speaks to your heart are you obeying today? Maybe you have a long-term goal of being a missionary to Haiti. Some of your short-term goals could be praying for Haiti, learning about the culture and language, going to Bible School, raising support. It is possible you want to be a teacher. Some of your short-term goals could be volunteering at children's club to see what age you enjoy teaching. Finding out what schools are best for the type of teaching career you want. God may have spoken to your heart to be a godly business leader. Which area of business? Is God calling you to work in the corporate world or an entrepreneur? A short-term goal could be going to a business school and working with a successful businessman.

Our vision must be more than a dream. It must become a reality and that will mean action. In the third volume of this series "Start To Finish" I discuss in detail these subjects. There are steps to take for the fulfillment of every vision and we are just dreamers, until we start implementing our plan with practical steps. There are far too many people who sit around and dream all of their lives. You must begin to walk. Maybe you are scared of going the wrong way. Well, if you have ever driven an automobile, then you will know it is much easier to turn and direct it while moving, than when it is sitting still. Start moving and if you are off course the Holy Spirit will align you as you go.

Some people talk about taking blind steps of faith. Well faith is not blind. Faith is always based upon having knowledge concerning the will of God. Faith's foundation is the word. The Bible is God's word: however, "faith is out of the source of that which is heard" (Rom. 10:17 Wuest). To understand vision, we must be able to hear God's word to us. As we read the word of God and listen to the preaching of the word, faith will arise in our hearts, to see God's hand move in our lives.

The Bible gives us what I will call the general will of God. That means we receive faith, to do God's will, by spending time in the word of God. However, it is the Holy Spirit who gives us specific direction for our lives. One of the gifts God has given to His church is that of the prophet. One of the functions of the prophet is to teach us to hear what the Holy Spirit is saying. Prophets are also gifted with the word of knowledge, word of wisdom and gift of prophecy to speak to individuals, churches and even nations about destiny and direction.

The Bible does not specifically tell us to be a business leader. How do you know what college to go to or even to go to college? We don't need a word about everything, but when it comes to major decisions in our lives and churches we need to listen to the Holy Spirit's direction. I am not saying that a prophet is going to tell you what you should do because that is divination. I am saying that you need to learn to listen to the Spirit of God for yourself who wants to direct your steps. The direction of the Spirit will be God speaking quietly to our heart, sound counsel from others or a prophetic word. A person with the gift of prophecy may help you to understand the voice of the Spirit and confirm certain things in your life, but you are not to look to them for direction.

It is only through the work of the Holy Spirit, that we can know which direction to take in our race. Paul encouraged Timothy to wage a good warfare "**according to the prophecies previously made concerning him.**" (I Timothy 1:18) Paul was telling Timothy to stand in faith, on the foundation of what God had said, concerning his purpose in life.

Writing down what God has spoken to our hearts and then speaking that out over our lives, brings us into agreement with God.

We need to be motivated and directed by the plans of God. Faith has action. As we allow the word of faith to activate and motivate our hearts we will practically apply God's word in our daily lives, which will cause us to succeed in life.

DEFINING SUCCESS AND PROSPERITY

Success and prosperity are terms that any North American has heard all of his life. In these times that we live in it seems that America is built on being prosperous and successful. As Christians, we need to be able to live in our culture, yet at the same time fulfill the will of God.

I like what William H. Cook has said:

> [15] "A right definition of success is important from two sides—from the side of having God in it, and from the side of having achievement in it. Defining success without having God in the definition leaves man without the blessing of God upon his life. Yet having God in the life and still not achieving is adding insult to the Infinite."

I want to give you my definition of what I call biblical success. **Success is completing and fulfilling the will of God for your life.** It is not having a million dollars, houses, cars or anything you want. It is laying hold of God's purpose and running the race He has set before you.

Success is not a smooth rosy road. Jesus was the most successful person to ever live yet he was crucified! Yes, he rose from the dead as the Victor; yet in this world's view of Him he was a failure. However, even today, there are millions partaking of his success every day.

If any other man was a biblical success it was Paul the apostle. Paul gave us his résumé for biblical success in II Corinthians 11:22-

27. He had to endure many difficulties; yet he continued to be obedient to the 'heavenly vision' for his life. It seemed that by the end of Paul's life, all of his work was under attack and he wound up in jail to be killed. However, we partake of his success even today, as we read and study his writings.

Was John the prophetic-apostle successful as he sat in that prison cell on the isle of Patmos writing the book of Revelation? In the worlds eyes no, but in God's eyes yes!

It was this same John who defined biblical prosperity for us. The scripture most often taken out of context, when speaking about prosperity is III John 2, **"Beloved, I pray that you may prosper in all things and be in health, just as your soul prospers."** The Greek word used for prosper here is *euodoō* and its meaning is *"to help on one's way or journey."* The problem is that many have interpreted the Bible through their cultural preference. We can't make the Bible fit our lifestyle, but we must let the Bible define our lifestyle. True biblical prosperity is not focused upon money, but upon fulfilling the purpose of God.

God desires us to prosper, yet biblical prosperity can be taught on any continent and in any nation on the face of the earth. I define prosperity as **"having enough to accomplish the will of God"**. You need prosperity to have success on your journey. Yes, this means you will need money but prosperity is more than money. Prosperity includes everything you will need to help you fulfill the purpose of God for your life and have a successful journey while in this body.

I could give you many examples from my personal life when God has prospered me as I have been walking by faith in His will. One such example is when my wife and I first moved to Canada. When we arrived we had no money and only the clothes in our suitcases. In a short time the Lord opened a door for us to be the leaders of a small church. One of the big problems we had was that we had no vehicle.

As my wife and I were praying during this time the Holy Spirit told my wife to put an ad in the Thrifty-Nickel for a car. She told me what the Lord directed her to do and I skeptically said to obey the leading of the Lord. She put an ad stating "Couple needing someone to sow a car into our ministry." Saturday came and no call, Sunday and then Monday the phone rang. I answered the phone and a Filipino man said, "I am calling concerning your ad in the paper. Tell me about the ad." I did. Then he said that his job was transferring him to Michigan in one week and he with his wife had been praying about what to do with an extra car they had. They had been praying about giving it to a ministry but didn't know where. He said he saw the ad in the paper and it just lit up. Well, he gave us the car before he left for Michigan. This was not a Cadillac but a Toyota. However, it was prosperity for us. It was a car that ran well and we could afford the insurance.

I was once listening to Clark Taylor, who is a church planting apostle from Australia. He was relating a story, which one of his Bible students from Papua New Guinea told him. This Bible student had finished school and went back to Papua New Guinea to pastor a church. As a pastor he was not making enough money to feed his family. He was praying to God about the situation he was facing. While walking on the beach and praying, a large fish washed upon the shore right in front of him. This was enough food to feed his family for a week. Amazing, but true!

God can provide in any wilderness you find yourself walking through. During my first years of Bible school I was taught a most important truth. **"Where God guides He provides!"**. The true biblical principles of prosperity and success can work anywhere on earth. It doesn't take a capitalistic system to prosper and succeed. It takes a determined faith to walk in the will of God!

I could give you many such examples of God prospering my family and I, so that we could get along in our journey in fulfilling His will. I am sure you have your own examples of how you have experienced God's provision, so that you could complete His will. His provision does not always come in a spectacular way, but in many cases God meets needs in a very practical manner. It may be a raise on your job or someone blessing you with gifts or groceries. God wants each of us to prosper and have success living our faith day to day, so that we can fulfill the vision He has placed before us.

It is God's desire to prosper you. If you are a parent, don't you want to do all you can do, to see that your children make it in life?

Our Heavenly Father desires to walk with us and help us in our race. If we will lay hold of His vision for our lives and be willing to follow Him with all of our heart, He will see to it that His plans are successful for our lives. Jeremiah says that He has a future, a hope and an expected end for us. Let us lay hold of His vision for our lives.

CHAPTER 5

How Can You Run Straight When You're Going Two Ways?

"Each one is tempted when he is carried away and
enticed by his own lust."
James 1:14

[16] "An old Greek fable says that the swift-footed
goddess Atlanta challenged her suitors to race with
her, with herself as the prize or death as the penalty
for losing.   Many competed and lost their lives.
Finally, a man named Hippomenes carried with him
three golden apples and entered the contest.   As
with the others, Atlanta swiftly passed him, but he
threw a golden apple.   She, startled, stopped to pick
it up.   He regained the lead but soon Hippomenes
again saw himself gradually slipping behind; and
again he threw a golden apple.   Atlanta, charmed by
its glitter, delayed to seize it, and fell behind.   But
once again, as they neared the goal, she was about to
pass him, and Hippomenes threw his last golden
apple.   Atlanta, lured by its charm, stopped again –
and lost the race."

This is just a Greek legend, however today we see the enemy to
our souls throwing these three golden apples to take us off
course as we run. They are: "the lust of the eyes, the lust of the
flesh, and the pride of life" (I John 2:16). Multitudes of Christians

today are being turned aside from full obedience to the will of God by Satan's "three golden apples"!

As disciples, whatever keeps us from running a straight course needs to be cut off from our lives, so that we are not hindered. The author of Hebrews talks about this, when he tells us to deal with the sin that so easily trips us up and takes us off course (Hebrews 12:1). He then instructs us that the way to deal with our sin is by looking unto Jesus who is supposed to be the pattern of our lives.

The Bible says that Jesus was tempted just like us. Jesus was tempted in the areas of the lust of the flesh, lust of the eyes and pride of life. The whole goal behind the Tempter is to cause us to take his bait. If we take Satan's bait, then it will take us down a course other than the one God has designed for us. We can look at Jesus and see that the Tempter tempted him yet He remained on course. Let's learn from His example!

At this point you are going to say, well that was Jesus, who was God manifested in human flesh. I am different! I will admit that there is a difference between our state and the state Christ was in, when He was tempted. He was untainted by sin and we are tainted; however, the Bible says that Jesus was tempted in all the same ways in which we are tempted. Bob Mumford in his book, 'The Purpose of Temptation' says:

> [17]"Though the temptation in the wilderness and the possibility of disobedience was real, Jesus, being sinless, did not have a sinful nature to which Satan could appeal. Tempted in all manner like as we, Jesus nevertheless was without sin. His temptation was indeed like ours, yet He was without the evil inclination."

Though Jesus was a man, he was a man without sin. We like Him are men, yet we live in unredeemed bodies that are still subject to the weaknesses of a fallen creation. As sons of God, we have received a new divine nature with the Spirit of Christ living in us, but we still live in an age of excess and temptation. Let's examine the three areas in which Satan in the wilderness tempted Jesus, because if we will examine these, it will help us to understand the main areas in which Satan appeals to us. He knows man and since he is the god of this age, he has devised such a system, which is very alluring to appeal to our 'lower nature'.

In the wilderness, Satan came to Jesus with his three golden apples. As I said in chapter 2, the wilderness is a training ground. Many Christians don't want to walk through the wilderness, but the pathway of a true disciple will always lead through the wilderness. The course, the Spirit of God led Jesus on, was straight into temptation, and every true disciple will have to follow the Pattern Son if he or she wants to finish their race. If we embrace the wilderness as disciples, then it will be a place of growing strong. It's only by walking through the wilderness, that we learn how to submit the areas in our own hearts that have not been completely surrendered to the cross.

THE LUST OF THE FLESH

The first area, in which Jesus was attacked, was the area of his fleshly lust or as I John 2:12 calls it the **'lust of the flesh'**. Why do I say this? Because the tempter said, **"If you are the Son of God, tell this stone to become bread"** (Luke 4:4). Jesus had been fasting for 40 days without food. Jesus was a man and his hunger pains were very real, not to mention the feelings of fatigue and discomfort he had in his body. This was a very real temptation to appeal to his appetite and lust.

I understand that Jesus was not tempted sexually in this context, but if you will examine the Bible, you will see that food and sex are inextricably tied together. Paul in I Corinthians 10:7 exhorts us, to not follow the pathway of the children of Israel in the wilderness, who continually yielded to the 'lower nature' and the world. It says that when Moses went up on Mt. Sinai to receive the law of God, the children of Israel, *"sat down to eat and drink, and stood up to play."* The term "play" here, as *The Expositor's Bible Commentary* brings out, means "drunken, immoral orgies and sexual play." They ate the food sacrificed to the golden calf and then many indulged in a sexual orgy in accordance with the pagan cult practices.

We are probably all familiar with the story of how Esau sold his birthright for a bowl of lentil stew. When the author of Hebrews mentions this story, it is interesting how he comments about Esau and the context in which it was written. In mentioning him, the author then exhorts us to not be an **"immoral or godless** person like Esau, who sold his own birthright for a single meal" (Hebrews 12:16). The Greek word for immoral is fornicator, which is someone who has illicit sex. The person who fornicates is thinking only about instant gratification. In the same way, Esau had more regard for the instant gratification, which came by fulfilling his natural desires than the will of God.

If we do not control our appetites then they will destroy us. This is what Paul said in Philippians 3:18. **"Many walk, of whom I often told you, and now tell you even weeping, that they are enemies of the cross of Christ; whose end is destruction, WHOSE GOD IS THEIR APPETITE"** (Emphasis Mine). All of us have the God-given appetites for both food and sex. They are given to man for his enjoyment, however when they began to rule our lives, we have stepped over into the realm of idolatry and whether knowingly or unknowing are in opposition to God.

As I have ministered many times in rehabilitation centers, I always tell them that any addiction, whether it is food, alcohol, drugs, or sex; *all have their roots in the lust of the flesh.* Addiction is simply when the 'unspiritual nature' is ruling the life of a person. If you take just a quick glance at the Bible, it is not hard to notice that many good people have fallen because they did not control their appetites. At the same time, you can look at the modern church and it is obvious that Satan has taken down many good men and women because of their refusal to deal with the lust of their flesh.

When we look at civilization, as a whole we have to notice that one of the main issues that men and woman must face is their sexuality. This does not matter if you live in the Outback of Australia, the Plains of Africa or in Modern Europe. Individuals will have to face their sexuality sooner or later. In modern civilization, it is not hard to notice the immoral sexual orientation of society, which has affected every continent.

With the birth of the Sexual Revolution in the 60's and 70,s we are now daily flooded with sexual innuendos. At all levels of society and in all cultures, we have been bombarded with talk and demonstration about sex. The entertainment media, commercial advertising are brimming over with it. Consider the curriculum being used in some of our schools.

We are seeing the effects of sexual immorality at all levels of society and in all cultures around the world. Abortion has become a holocaust; single parent mothers and even fathers are common, Aids is becoming the 20th century world plague, which all amounts to a total eroding of the foundations of civilization.

At the same time, American culture has become obsessed with food. Try a few experiments to discover how much food is a part of your life. I am not talking about the necessity to live; I am talking about the indulgence of the flesh.

The first experiment; fast without foods for a few days and then tell me how many times you are confronted with food advertising. You will be amazed at how many times you are encouraged to eat something, just to indulge yourself.

The second experiment; take a trip to a third world country and then upon your return, see if you discover any over emphasis placed upon eating in our culture.

We must eat and it is okay to enjoy our food. I like a good meal! My wife and I love to eat food from all different cultures. We love Indian, Mexican, Greek, Lebanese and the list could go on. God never said we could not enjoy food. In fact, food is for our enjoyment, but we must never let food fill a place in our hearts, which belongs to God. Sex is also to be enjoyed within the boundaries of the marriage bed, yet there are even times when married couples should abstain from food and sex for seasons of prayer (I Corinthians 7:5).

Our culture has been bombarded with ungodly attitudes toward food and sex. How much control we have over ourselves in these two areas, is a barometer to see how much our appetites rule over us. Having an uncontrolled appetite is one of the things that are destroying America and it is affecting the church in America. It is because we are eating Satan's golden apples and refusing to eat God's word, concerning the way we must discipline our bodies.

THE LUST OF THE EYES

The second area, in which Jesus was attacked, was the area of the lust for power or as I John 2:12 calls it the **'lust of the eyes'**. The eyes are what motivate our vision. Satan came to Jesus and **"he led Him up and showed him all the kingdoms of the world in a moment of time. And the devil said to Him, 'I will give you all this domain and its glory; for it has been handed over to me, and I give it to whomever I wish. Therefore if you worship before me, it shall all be yours'"** (Luke 4:5-7). This was truly a golden apple because money is one of the things that the world worships, because it rules the kingdoms of the world.

Earthly kingdoms have always been ruled by whoever possessed the power of monetary exchange. Is the glory of New York City the theatre shows in Times Square or the New York Stock Exchange? New York has been the capital of the world for the last 50 years because of the monetary exchange going on at Wall Street. *The accumulation of wealth is the accumulation of power.*

At the height of every great empire in history, has been a leader or group of people who have possessed the wealth through which they retained their power. If you owned the gold, then you controlled the military, religious leaders and governmental power. This is why Paul the apostle said that 'the love of money' is at the root of all kinds of evil.

Money is not evil! We all need money to live this life. However, when the sole purpose for our existence is the attaining of wealth we have departed from the faith and are on a quest for power. Jesus said it is possible to gain the world and lose our soul. I have seen people, who were once on fire for the things of God, slowly lose their zeal as money gained their undivided attention.

Just after I was born again, the Lord really began to deal with me about my affection for money. You see as a drug dealer I gained quite a love affair with money. I was instantly delivered from drugs, but the love of money took some time for me to part with. I still had several thousands of dollars in the bank and some other items, which I had purchased with drug money. It seemed that every time I was touched by the Holy Spirit He would move upon my heart and have me give much more than I wanted to give in the weekly offering. It took only a few months and I realized that I had given all of my money away! At the same time, during this process, the Lord removed the root of the love for money from my heart, however it is still an ongoing work that I have to keep an eye on.

How we relate with money reflects the way we relate with God. In speaking about money Jesus said, **"Where your treasure is, there will your heart be also."** If you have a problem with money, then deal with it and get your heart in the right place.

THE PRIDE OF LIFE

We can see that the last time the devil came to Jesus he led Him to Jerusalem. The devil took Him to the pinnacle of the temple, and said to Him, **"If you are the Son of God, throw yourself down"** (Luke 4:9). This temptation came in a different form. This was not an appeal to power or to meet a physical need, but an appeal to His pride or vanity and ego. I John 2:15 define it as the **'pride of life'**. Pride is simply going another way than the way of the Lord. Pride can be blinding because many times we can think we are doing God's will, but we are actually opposing Him. Think of the religious leaders who had Jesus crucified. When pride gets a root in our heart we begin to think more highly of ourselves than we should. The deception of pride is that we try to be something that we were not created to be.

There was a godly king of Judah named Uzziah, of whom it was recorded that **'he did right in the sight of the Lord.'** God gave him great victories in battle, however it says, **"when he became strong,** *his heart was so proud that he acted corruptly,* **and he** was unfaithful to the Lord" (II Chronicles 26:16). His pride caused him to do what was forbidden for him to do and that was entering the temple and burn incense before the Lord.

Under Old Covenant Law it was ordained for only the priest to burn incense. Uzziah in insolence against the Lord and His priest entered the sanctuary and "with a censer in his hand for burning incense, was enraged; and while he was enraged with the priests, the leprosy broke out on his forehead before the priests in the house of the Lord" (II Chronicles 26:19). Uzziah's success went to his head and it brought him down. Over confidence is an open door to the devil! When we get to the place where we think that nothing can stop us, because we have been successful, we are on the edge of destruction.

David committed his most serious transgression against the Lord just after a series of great successes. II Samuel 11:1 says that, "in the spring, at the time when kings go off to war, David sent Joab out with the kings men and the whole Israelite army. They destroyed the Ammonites and besieged Rabban. But David remained in Jerusalem." Did David become too comfortable in his success? Did pride begin to set in upon David's heart causing him to put his guard down? It is quite possible since it is in the very next verse, that we see David taken captive by the snare of Bathsheba's beautiful body. This was one of David's darkest moments. It is interesting that it was also David who wrote, "O how the mighty have fallen".

You are never too big to fall off of your horse! If you look throughout the Old Testament the horse is a symbol of trusting in the ability of man. It is leaning on the arm of flesh and departing from faith towards God. Every time we begin to trust in our own ability more than God's ability in us we will depart from our true purpose and are headed for a fall due to the arrogance of our hearts.

Under the Old Covenant, the kings of Israel were given three prohibitions. Deuteronomy 17:16-17 says that they, "shall not multiply horses for HIMSELF (the pride of life)...neither shall he multiply wives for HIMSELF (the lust of the flesh)...nor shall he greatly increase silver and gold for HIMSELF (the lust of the eyes)" (Emphasis Mine). Solomon extravagantly broke all three of these prohibitions and these three areas led to his demise.

The power of the 'unspiritual nature' is the pride of life. It is man-taking credit for what God has done. When God brought the Israelites into the land of Canaan, He warned them to not forget how they conquered the land. He told them about how they were going to be blessed and then said: **"When you have eaten and are satisfied, you shall bless the Lord your God for the good land which He has given you. BEWARE LEST YOU FORGET THE LORD YOUR GOD...AND YOUR HEART BECOMES PROUD"** (Deut. 8:10-14; Emphasis Mind). It is pride that led to the eventual downfall of the nation of Israel. They forgot it was God who gave them the power to accomplish all they did and that it was only because of His blessing that they experienced success. Pride will cause us to leave our first priority, which is God.

The pride of life is a snare, which will take us out of the place that God has given us as an inheritance. We must follow the example of Jesus and stay true to the purpose, which God has created us to fulfill. We don't have to prove anything. We only have to be what we were made to be and do what we were created do.

Jesus did not have to prove He was the Messiah by a self-proclaimed miracle. His calling was to obey the Father and do what He told Him to do. If the devil can get us into pride, then we will be taken out of the race and frustrate ourselves, our families and the will of God.

TEMPTATION AND TESTING

In the scenario that took place between Jesus and the devil, we see two things taking place. Jesus was being **tempted** by the devil, yet at the same time He was being **tested** or proven by the Father. There is a clear distinction between temptation and testing, yet many times they are taking place at the same time!

What was the devil trying to accomplish in tempting Jesus? The original Greek word for devil is *diabolos*. It is defined as one who falsely accuses and divides people. The devil was attempting to divide the Father and the Son just as he divided Adam and Eve from God in the Garden (Gen. 3:1-6). The serpent divided Adam and Eve in the garden by speaking a lie to Eve that she received, believed in her heart and then acted upon. Instead of staying true to the word like Jesus did, Eve believed a lie and was taken captive by the devil.

Let me give you an example. When I was a youth pastor in Up-State New York I was taking the youth group on a trip in the church van. At this time, I was also a professional driver and I always charted out my course in my mind before I drove, so I would know where I was going. I had gone down this road before and knew the route. I had clarity of vision and understanding about where I was going.

I then made a turn on the road that I knew I was supposed to make. I had been that way before, however all of a sudden the youth group, playing a trick on me, began telling me I had gone the wrong direction. At first I just ignored them, but as I began to meditate on what they had said I began to doubt and became unsure of myself. Nonetheless, I really was going in the right direction but because I listened to the other voice, which was a lie, it caused confusion and double-mindedness in me until I took the thought captive and stayed on course. I was a professionally tested driver; therefore I stayed true to my training and instincts, which kept us going the right way. This may seem like a silly and simple example, but this exact scenario goes on in the mind of a believer all the time.

The realm of operation, by which the devil operates through this world system, is temptation. A temptation is simply the deceptive schemes of the enemy twisting reality in such a way that a person is entangled into sin. This causes the person to walk and live in a way, which is contrary to God's will for his life.

As the world of virtual reality becomes more accessible to society, can you imagine what kind of a hay day demons are going to have. Satan loves to produce false illusions. He was the inspiration behind LSD and the song "Imagine", which was composed by the Beatles. He desires to be a creator like God, but the best he can come up with is a temporary illusion, which fades into eternal darkness.

Sin only brings temporary pleasure, and then the poison sets in to bring death. Powers of darkness through this world system are continually thrusting arrows of temptation at our mind, wills and emotions to cause us to become double-minded concerning the purpose of God. If we take the bait of temptation then it can cause us to love the world or set our affections on the world, then our faith will be quenched and we are double-minded about which direction to take in life.

Many people are confused about the difference between temptation and testing as to their source. James 1:13 says **"let no one say when he is tempted, 'I am being tempted by God'; for God cannot be tempted by evil, and He Himself does not tempt anyone.'"** Temptation comes from this present world order in opposition to God and those powers of darkness dominating it, which entice the lust of our flesh. However, in the midst of every temptation, God is also testing you. As long as we are in this world we are going to go through the wilderness of temptation. We need to view temptations as an opportunity to see any area in our hearts, which need to be given over completely to Him. It is in the midst of every temptation that the Holy Spirit is reminding us of what God has said to us, through His word and if we will use the word of God as a sharp sword, we can overcome any temptation.

Proverbs 8:1-2 is what I call the 'Crossroads of the Heart'. Here, we see wisdom calling out where the paths meet. In life, our paths will meet with temptation. Practically everyday of your life, you will have choices to make; to listen to wisdom or your own fleshly desires. I Corinthians 10:13 tells us **"no temptation has come your way that is too hard for flesh and blood to bear. God can be trusted to not allow you to suffer any temptation beyond your powers of endurance. He will see to it that every temptation has its way out, so that it will be possible for you to bear it"** (J.B. Phillips). At first glance, this text would seem to say that it is God who is doing the tempting. However, it simply says that we cannot be tempted to do evil with anything, which God has not provided a way of escape for through Jesus Christ.

In every temptation, it says that God provides a way out, so that we don't have to sin and be taken captive by the snares of the enemy. Every time Jesus was tempted, He referred back to the reference point of **"it is written."** The world says it is okay to sleep with your girlfriend. However, **"it is written"** in I Thessalonians 4:3-4 that, **"This is the will of God, your sanctification; that is, that you abstain from sexual immorality; that each of you know how to possess his own vessel in sanctification and honor."** A little money from the register won't hurt. However, **"it is written"** in Ephesians 4:28 to, **"Let him who steals steal no longer."**

If we want to find the way of escape in the midst of temptation, then we must rely on the tested and tried word of God. The word of God has been tested and proven. The word is more than just the scriptures, but it is the very person of Christ living in us. If we will stay united to the word when temptation comes, then we will pass the test! How did I stay on course when all the voices in the van were telling me I was going the wrong way? I stayed on course, because I stayed true to the information, I knew to be the truth. Many times it will feel like you are wrong, because everything will be going against you, but we must become solidly fixed on the truth of God's word. Face it, as a disciple of Christ; you are swimming up stream in this world. God's ways are not the world's ways!

As long as we live in this world, our faith will be tested on a continuous basis with the fires of temptations, persecution and trials (James 1:2). Temptation comes to appeal to our 'lower nature' and solicit us to do evil. At the exact same time, God is testing His word in you.

The word of God will give you the power you need to overcome any temptation and so prove (test) yourself to be a child of God. This is why the author of Hebrews could say; I am **"convinced of better things concerning you (Hebrews 6:9)."** I am convinced that if you hide God's word in your heart, it will clear your way, so that you can run your race. You must stay true to who you are, an overcoming child of God, so that you are not deceived as Eve who stumbled and fell. If you stumble and fall then I am convinced that you will repent and hide God's word in your heart so that you can keep running. We are all going to stumble, but you can't keep a disciple down.

REFUSING WISDOM COSTS

Temptation can only solicit us to evil, yet it is the evil desires in the soulish area of our hearts, which cause us to take the bait. James 1:14 says that we are **carried away** and **enticed by** *our own lust*. The Greek word for lust here is *epithumia*. It is defined as the active and individual desire resulting in *pathos* a Greek word meaning **the diseased condition of the soul**. You see, we all have areas in our soulish realm that have been damaged by our individual sin and the sin inflicted upon us by others. If these areas go without being healed, then when the right circumstances arise as a result of the temptations of the devil, we will be led away by them and taken captive.

Take for instance a young girl or boy who may have been damaged in their souls through the molestation of a relative or stranger. When that child reaches puberty and the right circumstances arise, that child will have a much stronger bent towards sexual sin, because of the diseased condition within the soul. A person who was raised in a home with arguing and yelling is going to have a stronger bent towards the sin of anger. It is statistically proven that those who grow up in the home of an alcoholic will have a higher likelihood of also becoming one. Not every person will have the same disease within their souls; however every soul born into Adam's race has been affected by evil desires.

If we refuse to deal with our ungodly lust, then they will take us into slavery. I find this is the main reason so many believers' live unfruitful lives and are still dominated by sin. When we refuse to deal with the evil desires in the soulish areas of our hearts it causes us to turn away from God.

I would have to say that if anyone knew about the depths of a backslidden heart, it would have to be Solomon. He instructed us in Proverbs 14:14 that **"the backslider in heart will have his fill of his own ways."** I don't know about you, but I don't want to be filled with my own ways.

It was Solomon who also said, **"there is a way that seems right to a man but its end is the way of death"** (Proverbs 16:25). It may seem appropriate to party with your co-workers after work in a place where there is adult entertainment and open sexual sin. You reason to yourself, "It's not like I party all the time. I just need to let my hair down." The path of least resistance may feel like the right thing to do at the moment; however it is a slippery slope that you cannot be assured to be able to climb back up. The famous last words are, "I thought I could handle just one night" or "I was only going to do it once."

Paul the apostle in writing to the church in Rome said that when we give ourselves to sin, we become its slave. Although sin is not supposed to be our master it still can be. If we begin to serve sin, we will pay the price for that servitude. If we refuse to listen to wisdom then it leads to a life of slavery. If we begin to see our lives dominated by sin, then it is time to make a radical cut. As disciples, we have been called to live a life dominated by the Spirit God, not by slavery of our ungodly desires.

MAKE A RADICAL CUT

It has been my observation that one reason we live in slavery to sin is because we have become friends with that which is holding us down. What happened to Samson? He put his head in the lap of the harlot, one too many times. He became comfortable with what desired to take his strength and destroy him! Let's face it sin is attractive, but we are in a dangerous place when we become comfortable with sin. The dangerous thing about this, is the sin we are holding on to so closely, is the very thing bringing death into our lives.

Jesus has given us solutions for dealing with areas in our lives. He brought some radical thinking to this area. He said:

"And if your hand causes you to stumble, cut it off; it is better for you to enter life crippled, than having your two hands, to go into hell, into the unquenchable fire, [WHERE THEIR WORM DOES NOT DIE, AND THE FIRE IS NOT QUENCHED.] And if your foot causes you to stumble, cast it out; it is better for you to enter the kingdom of God with one eye, than having two eyes, to be cast into hell."   (**Mark 9:43-47**)

Michael L. Brown in his book "Go And Sin No More" comments on this text by saying,

[18]"There are few things more radical than amputation. Doctors cut off hands, feet, or legs as a last resort when all else has failed. They do it because they have no choice. If they don't, the infection will spread, destroying the whole body. So it's either one limb that goes or the whole body that dies. And once the amputation is done, it can't be undone. Once the limb is severed it will never be used again. Yet, Jesus tells us to amputate our hands or feet if they cause us to sin."

No, don't go out and buy a saw. Jesus, as He did so well, was using a radical word picture to tell us a radical message that we cannot serve two masters. You cannot be a slave to sin and serve God with your whole heart at the same time, you have to radically deal with that which is bringing death into your life.

James poses a question in his epistle. **"Do you not know that friendship with the world is hostility toward God? Therefore whoever wishes to be a friend of the world makes himself an enemy of God."** How do we become a friend of the world? We become the world's friend when we begin to love the world. The

Greek word John uses in I John 2:15 in telling us to not love the world is *agapaō* and it means to set our affection upon something. The Lexical Aids to the New Testament literally says that this word "indicates a direction of the will".

When we begin to set our affection upon this world more than God, then our pathway is diverted which will begin to affect [19] "what we do (our hands), where we go (our feet) and how we view things (our eyes)". This is biblical idolatry! An idol is something we give our time to, our money to and set our affections upon.

What are some of the things that modern man idolizes? Money, sports, occupation, human body, sex, food, possessions, entertainment, and the list could go on. None of these things are necessarily bad in themselves but when they become the center of our attention, they can become idols in our lives. We have become friends of this world and put ourselves in opposition to God because our affections have been captivated. When our priorities have pushed God out of our lives and we have put other things as the center of our attention it is time to make adjustments. In a practical way, how do we cut off our hands and feet or pluck out our eyes and throw them away, so that Jesus takes first place in our lives?

It is not the physical members of our body, which is the root of our problem; these areas have just become the vehicle or instrument of sin in our lives. In Romans 6 where Paul was talking about slavery to sin he said, **"do not let sin reign in your mortal body that you should obey its lusts, and do not go on presenting the members of your body to sin as instruments of unrighteousness."** If Paul was telling us to do something, then he obviously had a solution. He said that we don't have to be dominated by sin and our lives don't have to obey the lusts in the soulish area of our hearts. We can be free to serve God with our whole heart, but we must bring those areas affected with disease to the healing power of the cross. Just as a doctor will not operate on you without your consent, so you must present yourself to God as a willing sacrifice.

God's operating tool for surgically removing disease from our souls is His sharp two-edged sword. Hebrews 4: 12 says that

"The word of God is living and active and sharper than any two-edge sword, and piercing as far as the division of soul and spirit, of both joints and marrow, and able to judge the thoughts and intentions of the heart."

It is the living word of God that will pierce our hearts and heal our wounds. I Peter 2:11 says **"abstain from FLESHLY LUSTS, which wage war against the soul."** Peter uses this same Greek word *epithumia* and he shows us that there can be no co-existence with fleshly lusts. If you want to possess your Promised Land, then you must allow the Holy Spirit to take the word of God and cleanse those areas in your heart that have been wounded. As long as we allow our fleshly lust to direct our affections then our pathway will be diverted.

The children of Israel were prone to following their own fleshly lusts as they wandered around in circles for 40 years in the wilderness. There was a whole generation, which never fulfilled their intended purpose. Paul told us to learn from their mistakes in I Corinthians 10:1-14.

It is not until Joshua circumcised the new generation of warriors, that they rose up and conquered the Promised Land. Joshua 5:4 says, **"all the people who came out of Egypt who were males, all the men of war, died in the wilderness along the way." It was their children whom God raised up and Joshua circumcised them "for they were uncircumcised."** Can you imagine a whole army of men, not newborn babies being circumcised? This must have been a bloody mess and very humiliating. However, they could not be God's warriors until they had submitted to the covenant sign of circumcision.

If we want to possess our Promised Land in the power of God, then we must humble ourselves in humility before Him. Our identification in Christ is tied to our covenant relationship with

Him. I John 5:8 speaks of "the Spirit, the water and the blood." I refer to this as the threefold cord of the covenant.

The blood of the covenant must be applied to our lives, as we totally identify with the cross and follow Him. Under the Old Covenant the Mosaic Law was written in stone, however in Christ "the Spirit of the living God" puts His power and desires in our hearts (II Corinthians 3:3). As we live, work and play we will get the dirty residue of this world on us affecting our view of Christ in us; therefore we must be daily washed off by renewing our souls with the water of the word of God (Ephesians 5:25). Then Paul in Colossians 2:11 says our baptismal identification with Christ is like circumcision and sets us free from the 'lower nature'. The threefold cord of covenant is about partnering with the ability of Christ to bring us into all that God has for us.

Just as the children of Israel were commanded to eradicate their enemies and possess their land, so we must also be tenacious enough, to not allow anything to keep us from God's purpose. We must turn away from the sin, which so easily causes us to stumble and totally identify with the freedom that is ours in Christ. It was Jesus who said, **"the kingdom of heaven is forcibly entered and violent men seize it for themselves"** (Matthew 11:12). No one can do it for you. You must seize hold of God's purposes for yourself. Is gossip, backbiting, gluttony, addiction, strife etc. controlling your life? If the works of the 'lower nature' (Galatians 5:19-21) are dominating your life then it is up to you to allow Christ to freely live His life in you.

Am I saying that we can be sinless? Is it possible to live a life without ever sinning? I believe if we take a balanced view of scripture, then we can say that it is impossible to be sinless (that is never committing a sin), yet we can live life without sin dominating and controlling our lives.

Just as the children of Israel did not defeat all of their enemies in one battle neither are you. We grow in Christ from glory to glory. Just as a tree grows in stages and is perfect in each stage so it is with our walk in Christ. The more you learn to yield to the Spirit of life then day by day you will find yourself living freely in the presence of the Father. We are going to have bad days, but that does not change who we have been made through our new birth nor does it change the Father's heart concerning us.

When we are made new creations and born of the Spirit of God at that moment we were brought into union with God's Spirit. Christ comes to live in our hearts by faith and we become partakers of His divine nature (II Peter 1:4). Although we are justified and reconciled to God, we still have areas in our souls or hearts that are affected by the 'lower nature'. This is where the conflict arises! In Galatians 5:17 Paul describes this by saying, **"the flesh sets its desire against the Spirit, and the Spirit against the flesh; for these are in opposition to one another, so that you may not do the things that you please."**

You see if we don't reckon the 'lower nature' dead, then it will cause us to be double-minded. This is the very reason we have so many unstable Christians! If our hearts are divided, we are literally trying to run two different directions, at the same time. I believe this is why so many Christians, sit in counseling offices, going around and around year after year without ever maturing or completing the will of God for themselves (I am in no way in opposition to biblical counseling). True biblical counseling is bringing someone to the truth of God's word.

I find it amazing that some teach that repentance is not something believers should do and is simply an action for the unbeliever in regards to initial conversion. II Corinthians 7:10 speaks of a godly repentance that leads to life. The Holy Spirit cannot make us repent of ungodly conduct, but He will convict us of sin and remind us of our identity in Christ (John 16:8). We have to humble ourselves and in humility receive God's word, implanted, which renews our souls (James 1:21).

Repentance is simply responding to the Holy Spirit's loving conviction, which draws us back to the Father. The Holy Spirit will remind us of the work of Christ on the cross and the commitment we have made to Him. Repentance is turning away from what has our attention and turning back to our covenant relationship or identity in Christ resulting in open fellowship with our Father. I John 1:9 says that "If we confess our sins, He is faithful and righteous to forgive us our sins and to cleanse us from all unrighteousness."

As disciples, there is only one pathway to follow and that is the path of the Pattern Son, who has gone before us. Jesus opened up His ministry being tempted in the wilderness, yet I believe it is in the Garden of Gethsemane that we see His greatest test. Frank Viola says, "In this episode, we discover the collision of two wills: the will of the human Jesus and the will of God the Father. In the end, as was His usual course, Jesus submitted His will to the will of His Father."

THE PATHWAY OF WISDOM

In the greatest wisdom book ever written, Proverbs, wisdom is portrayed as two women. One is a virtuous woman and the other is an insolent rebellious harlot. They are both presented as crying out for our attention. The harlot tries to gain our attention by appealing to our fleshly desires and the virtuous woman is gently persuading us to walk in the fear of the Lord. These two women are representative of two systems within the earth. The harlot being symbolic of the world and the kingdom of darkness by which it is empowered. It finds its ultimate fulfillment in the Babylon spoken of in Revelations 14, 17 and 18. The other is the virtuous woman, the bride of Christ, under the leadership of Jesus as the head. This woman speaks under the inspiration of the Holy Spirit to the hearts of men. The choice we have to make is whom are we going to pay attention too?

Just as in the wilderness, Jesus as a man was again faced with a decision to make in the Garden of Gethsemane and it is here that we gain a clearer understanding in overcoming temptation. It is in the Garden, that we learn the secret of yielding our lives to the Spirit of wisdom.

It is interesting to note that this is the same night in which Jesus partook of His last Passover with His disciples. Just as they finished the Passover and right before they entered the Garden, there arose a heated discussion about who was the greatest among them.

On the night of the Passover, Jesus gave a clear discourse on the difference between being self-serving and laying down our lives to serve. It is not the self-serving who are great in the kingdom but, those who pour out their lives to serve others. James describes the self-serving type of person as someone who has given him or herself over to demonic wisdom (James 3:13-16). When we are driven by demonic wisdom then it will always result in causing selfish-ambition, jealousy and strife. However, the wisdom flowing down from the Holy Spirit will bring unity of heart, which will produce an overflow of peace and the ability to work as a team member.

We all begin the Christian life absorbed within ourselves, but the only way we are supposed to be is as the Son of Man; **For even the Son of man came not to be ministered unto, but to minister, and to give his life a ransom for many** (Mark 10:45) Live as He did, not to be ministered unto, but to minister, to pour out. This is just what we find Jesus doing in the Garden and that is pouring out His life for others.

It is only because Jesus was willing to pour out His life that we could be saved. The cross was the product of Gethsemane, the direct result of surrender. Jesus Himself died on Calvary, but He died to Himself in Gethsemane. That is exactly what we see in the Gospel accounts of the Garden. We see the Son of God, Immanuel, God manifested in the flesh having a struggle with His own soul submitting to the will of God. It is here, that we see a distinction between the Father and Son. The 'mystery of the Godhead' comes to light in this portion of scripture, because we see the Son of God struggling to completely surrender to the will of the Father and the focal point of this struggle takes place in the soulish realm.

> "Then Jesus came with them to a place called Gethsemane, and said to His disciples, 'Sit here while I go over there and pray.' And He took with Him Peter and two sons of Zebedee, and began to

be grieved and distressed. Then He said to them, **My soul is deeply grieved to the point of death**; remain here and keep watch with me. And He went a little beyond them, and fell on His face and prayed, saying, 'My Father, if it is possible, let this cup pass from Me; yet not as I will, but as Thou wilt.' And He came to the disciples and found them sleeping, and said to Peter, "So, you men could not keep watch with Me for one hour? **Keep watching and praying; that you may not enter into temptation; the spirit is willing, but the flesh is weak.'** He went away again a second time and prayed, saying, 'My Father, if this cannot pass away unless I drink it, Thy will be done." **(Matt. 26:36-42)** (Emphasis Mine)

Jesus had His own will, but He lived His life totally submitted to the will of the Father. It is in Gethsemane, which means, 'wine press', that we see for the first time in scripture, a clear distinction between His will and the will of the Father. Jesus' soul was feeling great pressure because He was being faced with a complete and total absorption into God through death, burial and resurrection. This is the place so many of us surrender to the 'lower nature', instead of surrendering to the change the Holy Spirit is trying to bring in our hearts. However, it is just this place that God is trying to work His will into our hearts.

God uses pressure, to bring us to a place of decision, which causes our faith and our character to mature. We have to grow up into Christ and each stage of growth is perfect yet each stage of growth has its challenges. We must learn to press through tribulation. Romans 5:3-4 says to **"exult in our tribulations, knowing that tribulation brings about perseverance; and perseverance, proven character."** God is working on our character, so that we react as Christ would in the midst of every situation. The Greek word tribulation used in Romans 5 is the word *thilipsis*. It means to crush, press, compress, squeeze. God is literally trying to squeeze the life out of you.

[19]"We must learn God's methods, plans, and purposes. God's intent is not to take us OUT of pressure, but to lead us and bring us THROUGH pressure."

In Gethsemane, when pressure is applied, the real thing comes out. Have you ever been in a place of pressure, when all of sudden you started speaking foul language? All of a sudden things you thought you would never do you seem to be struggling with. God is letting you see what is in your heart! James speaking to born again Christians tells them to, **"Draw near to God and He will draw near to you, Cleanse your hands, you sinners; and purify your hearts, you double-minded."** The soulish areas of our heart begin to be delivered, healed and surrender to the Lord as we pray the prayer which Christ prayed in the Garden, "Not my will, but your will be done."

Jesus told us to seek first the kingdom of God. To be double-minded is to have two opinions. In the Garden, we see that Jesus had to bring His entire existence and submit it to the will of the Father. A united heart is a heart that has been unified through total surrender. It is the place where we totally identify with Christ and focus on His power at work within us. Christ maturing in us to where we consistently demonstrate His nature is our goal.

If we become a friend of the world, then we automatically become God's enemy. However, the good news is the Spirit of God is always drawing us back, so that we can run a straight course. We can't die to self through self-effort. We can't even change ourselves, but we can humble ourselves. James 4:5 says, **"do you think the Scripture speaks to no purpose; 'He jealously desires the Spirit which He has made to dwell in us?"** (King James) I like the way the New American Standard comments on this text by saying, **"The Spirit which He has made to dwell in us jealously desires us."** The Spirit of God doesn't want us to be wounded and taken off course. He doesn't like it when our affections are on the world.

The Spirit of Wisdom is always trying to persuade us to walk in the grace of God. He always points us to the crucified lifestyle, where we no longer live, but we are learning to let Christ live His life through us by faith. We can't overcome the enemy nor change ourselves, yet if we yield to the Spirit of Christ we can do everything He desires us to do. God gives grace to those who see their need. He will resist the self-serving and self-sufficient, until they're willing to fall on the rock. We must learn to humble ourselves and fall on the rock, by receiving with humility, what God's word says.

If we don't bend our knees in humility and prayer, then our pride will take us down, when temptation knocks on the door of our heart. When we refuse to submit to God, then we will not have the grace we need to accomplish His will. The rock will fall on the self-serving and self-sufficient and great will be that fall. Proverbs 29:1 speaks of such a person. **"A man who hardens his neck after much reproof will suddenly be broken beyond remedy."**

In I John 2:17 the apostle helps us gain a clear perspective on this world by saying, **"the world is passing away, and also its lusts (*epithumia*); but the one who does the will of God abides forever."** Accomplishing God's will for our lives is the most important thing in this life. It is up to us, if we want to partake of temporary lust and the passing pleasures of sin or experience the eternal will of God.

The Spirit of wisdom is calling out to all who will listen. The Holy Spirit is not out to condemn you because of your weaknesses, but He wants to come along beside you and strengthen you. It is a wise person who recognizes his weaknesses. It is only as we acknowledge our need, that we can be changed. The fear of the Lord is the beginning of wisdom. To fear God is to give Him his rightful place in our lives. If we will learn how to submit ourselves to God, then we will discover His power to resist the enemy in every situation. As we do this, we will run a straight course in the race of faith.

CHAPTER 6

Learning To Run From A Place Of Rest

"Let us then exert ourselves to enter that rest"

Hebrews 4:11

We had been meeting for early morning prayer every day as a group for almost a year and for the last week I had not noticed John in the group. I did not know him that well, but I had given him a ride home a few times after prayer. John was one of those individuals who pursued God with his whole heart. He was earnest in prayer. He was a man who was hungry for the things of God. He had great zeal, but I was soon to find out, it was not tempered with biblical wisdom.

As I was in prayer one morning, the Holy Spirit laid John upon my heart and I sensed a need to go visit him. I had some extra time that morning, so I stopped by his house and knocked on the door. I heard a voice from inside instructing me to come in. I stepped into the house and John was lying on the couch. I asked him how things were and he said 'I am resting'. By the way he said it I knew he didn't mean that he was tired and therefore he was resting. As I questioned him I discovered what he meant. John had heard a teaching about entering into the rest of God and as far as he was concerned, he was doing just that. He invited me to lie on the other couch and to enter into the rest of God. Naïve as I was, I did. We lay there on the couches listening to some relaxing music while praying and in our minds we had entered into the rest of God.

This story is an example of how zeal without sound biblical knowledge can lead to foolishness at best and heresy at worst. I am not saying that there is anything wrong with lying on a couch listening to relaxing music while praying. That is a good thing, yet it is not necessarily what entering into God's rest is all about. As we shall see, the rest of God is not a cessation of an active Christian life, but the very source of one.

It is the author of Hebrews who paints a word picture for us describing the rest of God. In the book of Hebrews we find the author contrasts the earthly ministry of Israel to the heavenly ministry of Christ. He shows us the superiority of the New Covenant and clearly portrays the Old Covenant ministries and promises as having been brought to completion and fulfillment in Christ. The law and prophets have been replaced by the true reality. The types and shadows, of which they spoke, are no longer the focus, because they have been consumed by the brightness of the glory of Christ (II Corinthians 3: 7-18).

In chapters 3 and 4 of Hebrews, we see a contrast between the children of Israel entering into the Promised Land of Canaan and believers entering into Christ. This is spoken of in the terminology of the rest of God. The 'rest' spoken of here is not taking a day off from work or spending a special day of the week worshipping God. It is a ceasing from our own carnal strivings and by faith entering into the resting place of God's promises and presence. It is entering into a personal relationship with a living personal God.

The reason we can enter into the rest of God is because God has entered into His and He is simply calling us to enter along with Him. Hebrews 4:4,10 says, **"God rested on the seventh day from all His works. THE ONE WHO HAS ENTERED HIS REST HAS HIMSELF ALSO RESTED FROM HIS WORKS, as God did from His"** (Emphasis Mine). We have become partakers of a complete and perfect salvation. The finished work of Jesus is the ground of our faith. In Andrew Murray's book, "The Holiest Of All", he tells us that:

> [20] "Because Christ has put away sin, rent the veil, and is seated at the right hand of the throne, - because all is finished and perfected, and we have received the Holy Spirit from heaven in our hearts to make us the partakers of the glorified Christ, we

may with confidence, with boldness, rest in Him to maintain and perfect His work in us."

I personally believe the reason very few people really understand the book of Hebrews is because they don't have a firm grasp on the basic milk of God's word. If we can simply get a firm grasp on the basics and take a radical look at the New Covenant it will help us understand what the word of God is teaching. There is nothing more basic than the revelation of 'Christ in you', yet it is a deep well, which we continually draw from for the rest of eternity. One author has rightly noted that, "true apostolic vision is Christ living in people - not buildings". If we look at scripture we will discover that entering into the 'rest of God' is simply understanding who we are in Christ. It then is understanding that He is in us and learning to allow Him by His power to work through our lives.

Jesus while he was walking on this earth beckoned the people by saying,

> "vs. 28 Come to Me, all who are weary and heavy-laden, and I will give you rest. vs. 29 Take My yoke upon you, and learn from Me, for I am gentle and humble in heart; and YOU SHALL FIND REST FOR YOUR SOULS. vs. 30 For My yoke is easy, and My load is light." (Matt. 11:28-30 Emphasis Mine)

The yoke is not a well-known instrument in modern days, however in ancient times the yoke was seen daily. A yoke was used to couple two animals together so that they could work. In the Old Testament the yoke is spoken of figuratively of severe bondage, or affliction, or subjection. In the New Testament, the word yoke is also used to denote servitude and Jesus told us to come under His yoke and to serve Him in humility of heart. When we partake of Christ's divine nature at new birth, we are then yoked to Him and we must learn how to become His co-laborer. It is only through learning how to cooperate with His ways that we will truly have productive lives in the kingdom of God.

Entering into the rest of Christ, will take our undivided attention. It is returning to a single focus of devoting our entire lives upon Christ. In Hebrews, we see that it is only those whose hearts are wholly given over to the Lord which are able to enter into His rest. **"For indeed we have had good news preached to us, just as they (the children of Israel in the wilderness) also; but the word they heard did not profit them, because it was not UNITED BY FAITH in those who heard"** (Hebrews 4:2; Emphasis Mine).

The first two foundational doctrines, which need to be laid down in our hearts, are repentance from dead works and faith towards God. The good news is that Christ has finished the work of our salvation. He partook of our humanity and has conquered Satan, sin, and death through His death, burial and resurrection. He has entered into heaven and is sitting at the right hand of the Father, as our High Priest, interceding for us and calling us up into a place of union with Him. Our hearts must become sensitive to the good news so the power of the endless life of Christ can now work in us.

Hebrews 4:9-10 says, **"There remains therefore a Sabbath rest for the people of God. For the one who has entered His rest has himself also rested from his works, as God did from His."** Right here, at the very beginning of our faith, so many people are tripped up. Far too many believers have had the faulty foundations of dead works laid down in their lives and they need foundation repair! They live in what I call the 'Cycle of Dead Works'. The very center of this cycle is a salvation based on self. They have never had a clear understanding of entering into the rest of God and ceasing from their own self-effort, by allowing Christ to work in them so that He can then work through them. Their lives have never been solidly founded completely upon Christ the foundation.

In Chapter 3 of this book, we discovered the word of the cross and the blood covenant. As I mentioned, the word of the cross covers not only the death of Christ, but also His burial and resurrection. Jesus not only died for our sins, but has also been raised up as the life-giving Spirit and from His throne emanates the power of an endless life.

We must come to know and experience the Heavenly Christ who has overcome the enemy and entered in for us. He sits upon a throne as our High Priest in power, keeping us in personal living fellowship with the Father, so that in Him, we too enter the rest of God. We must come to know Him, as our heavenly Joshua, following Him and allowing Him to bring us into our land of promise. It is only those who have the same spirit of faith, which Joshua possessed, that will be able to enter this place of endless power. Jesus never told us to follow Him in our own strength. He told us to take His yoke.

It is through the Spirit of God, that we are brought into union with Christ. The Holy Spirit is called the Helper in John 14:16. We need the Holy Spirit! He is the one Jesus sent to be with us and in us. Oswald Chambers writes, *"The Holy Spirit is the one who makes everything Jesus did for you real in your life."* We have been brought into union with the risen Christ, by the Spirit He has sent to be in us and with us. It is from this place of union or rest that we are able to live, move and have our beings in Christ. We must be diligent to put Christ on daily and enter into the yoke of His rest.

THE DISCIPLINED RUNNER NEVER FAINTS

It is only by faith that we are able to become partakers of all that Christ has done for us and wants to do in and through us. It is in Philippians 2:13 that Paul writes, **"my beloved, just as you have always obeyed, not as in my presence only, but now much more in my absence, WORK OUT YOUR SALVATION with fear and trembling;"** (Emphasis Mine) This is where far too many people stop reading. If you stop at the first part, you will never be able to accomplish the task, because it will be based upon yourself. I am sure that you have proven to yourself, as I have, that you are unable to neither save nor successfully change yourself. Paul goes on to say, "for IT IS GOD WHO IS AT WORK IN YOU, both to will and to work for His good pleasure."

If you grew up in America during the 1980's I am sure you heard the Army slogan, 'Be All You Can Be.' We need to have this same disciplined attitude, to become all we are destined to be in Christ. It is only those who learn to discipline themselves, who will be able to reach their full potential. It is the author V. Ramond Edman, who says,

> [21] "Ours is an undisciplined age. The old disciplines are breaking down...Above all, the discipline of divine grace is derided as legalism or is entirely unknown to a generation that is largely illiterate in the Scriptures. We need the rugged strength of Christian character that can come only from discipline."

The way many believers view church in our time has much in common with the tourist mindset. During the late 1990's and early 2000's, Westerners became world travelers like never before and the tourist industry experienced a big boom. At the same time, many believers have the same mentality. They make weekly trips to a building they call church while expecting all of their comforts and needs to be met by the professionally paid ministers. The mentality of the Western culture has found its way into far too much of the church where the people expect to be entertained and served.

The cruise ship mentality has captured far too much of the church. Christianity is not to be a self-centered life, but a commitment to follow Christ. We live in an instant society and everyone is in a hurry. We want instant spiritual growth; however spiritual growth does not happen during the highpoints experienced during vacations.

It is only through daily spiritual discipline that the new man, Christ in us, matures to become all that we can be. No one is born the best runner in the world; they must give themselves completely to the training and lifestyle of a runner. Although they may have been born with all the potential to be the best, it is only through training, that they are able to realize their full potential.

In reading the book of Hebrews it seems that the author gives us a contradiction in terms by telling us to be 'diligent to enter' into rest. When we think of the word rest we think of a cessation from activity. However, as you read the New Testament you will discover that we are co-laborers with Christ. As co-laborers we have a part to play. Jesus told us to take His yoke upon our lives. We are joined to Christ and enter into His rest, so that we can learn to allow His power and grace to help us bear all the fruit that we can.

Jesus said that apart from Him we could do nothing (John 15:5). You may say, well I can do a lot of things without Jesus and there are people in the world who do all kinds of things without Jesus. You are right; however we can do nothing of eternal value without Christ. When all is said and done, for the Christian, what is going to matter is did we do the will of the Father? Were we laboring out of the realm of the Spirit in union with Christ or the strivings of 'unspiritual nature' doing our own thing?

We must take upon ourselves the same attitude, which Christ possessed. He came for one reason and that was to accomplish His Father's will. He was willing to deny Himself so that God's desires could be accomplished through Him and we must discipline ourselves if we ever want to lay hold of that purpose. Being diligent to enter into the rest of God is practicing spiritual discipline to bring us into alignment with the finished work of Christ.

Runners must practice daily bodily discipline. Paul the apostle, instructed his spiritual son, Timothy to discipline himself for the purpose of godliness. We must take heed to this same instruction, because godliness or spiritual exercise **"is profitable for all things, since it holds promise for the present life and also for the life to come"** (I Timothy 4:7-8). The word translated 'discipline' in the New American Standard Bible is the Greek word *gumnasia* from which our English word gymnasium and gymnastics derive. This word means 'to exercise or discipline.' Practicing spiritual discipline on a daily basis is the pathway for entering into the rest of God and the development of the inward man, from which flows the purpose of God for our lives.

DISCIPLINING OUR BODIES

If we refuse to take up our cross and follow Jesus then we cannot be his disciples. True discipleship means cross bearing, however we need to see what it means to take up our cross. Is it wearing a big gold cross around our necks? What about taking a physical wooden cross and dragging it around wherever we go? None of these acts have anything to do with taking up our cross.

We have already seen in Chapter 3 of this book, that to take up our cross is to totally identify with Christ and His message. Our salvation is based upon identifying with the crucified and risen Christ, however it is through the biblical doctrine of baptisms, that we learn about this total identification.

In Hebrews 6:2, the Bible talks about "the doctrine of baptisms". Take note, that 'baptisms' is not singular, but plural. I believe the Bible teaches three main 'baptisms'. There are a number of other times the word baptism is used in the Bible, but I feel they could come under the category of the three main 'baptisms'. These three main baptisms are 'Baptism Into Christ's Body', 'Baptism Into Water' and 'Baptism Into The Holy Sprit'.

To be baptized into Christ's body happens when we accept Jesus Christ as our Lord and we receive the Holy Spirit. At the moment of new birth, by the renewing of the Holy Spirit, we are baptized or totally identified with Christ and become a part of His body. This is not a physical change, nor a physical act. It is the work of the Holy Spirit, which transforms our hearts. The apostle John calls this being **'born from above'**. Paul in II Corinthians 5:17 says we become **'new creations'**; in Titus 3:5 he calls it the **'washing of regeneration'**; in Ephesians 4:24 it is called the **'new man'**, and then in Galatians 3:27 he uses the term **'baptized into Christ'**. All of these terms basically mean the same thing. The basic meaning is that by the Holy Spirit, Christ takes up residence in our hearts.

To be 'baptized into Christ's body' means that Christ now lives in us. Paul says in II Corinthians 6:17 that **"we are the temple of the living God. As God said: "I will live in them and walk among them, I will be their God, and they will be my people"** (N.L.T.). Yet, it is through the biblical practice of 'baptism into water' that we begin to walk out the truth that Christ lives in us. [21]"Many in the church today see 'baptism into water' as just an added ritual on top of an already self-centered gospel". As you look at the book of Acts and the letters of Paul,

> [22] "Water baptism is given far more importance in the New Testament than the contemporary church has recognized. Our immersion in water is a ceremonial ritual meant to symbolize our commitment to make our total commitment to Jesus a reality, that we will no longer live for ourselves but for Him."

Water baptism, though it may be a one-time act, as disciples we must daily present our bodies to God, so that they can become the vehicle by which God's purpose can be done in the earth. Paul said, **"I buffet my body and make it my slave, lest possibly, after I have preached to others, I myself should be disqualified"** (I Corinthians 9:27). The call to discipleship is a call to master our bodies, so that they are used to fulfill God's purposes and bring glory to His name. Peter in his first epistle says:

> "Since Christ has suffered in the flesh, arm yourselves also with the same purpose, because he who has suffered in the flesh has ceased from sin, so as to live the rest of the time in the flesh **no longer for the lusts of men, but for the will of God."**
>
> (I Peter 4:1-2; Emphasis Mine)

As I have already stated, the sufferings we experience as disciples will come in the form of persecution, difficult situations, the denying of ourselves. You probably found out that when you made a commitment to Jesus Christ, you did not quickly find a crowd form to applaud your decision. You most probably experienced some form of persecution, unless your family and friends are all Christians. I doubt your unsaved friends and family members spontaneously gathered around you to offer congratulations. You're not alone! Multitudes, who have made a commitment to become Christ's disciple, have experienced opposition from earthly relationships.

I had a friend who did a series of meetings in India. There was one particular young man who made a radical commitment to Christ and was baptized into water. Two days later they found this young man dead in a well, killed by his own family.

Jesus demands we put Him first and everyone will not like you doing this. The very words of Christ say, **"he who loves father or mother more than Me is not worthy of Me: and he who loves son or daughter more than Me is not worthy of me"** (Matthew 10:37). Does this mean we treat our parents with disrespect, or have the right to neglect our children? No! What it is saying is that Jesus has first priority in our lives.

When we accepted Christ, we became a part of His body and at that moment He became the director of our lives. Are you living with your boyfriend? Do your close friends serve God? The reality is that whom you closely associate with is going to greatly affect your life. You can't live in sin with your boyfriend or girlfriend and serve God at the same time. You will have to give up one or the other. You can't constantly be around unbelievers with no Christian fellowship and expect it to not affect you. It is up to you to cut off relationships, which are going to hinder your walk with God and cultivate those that are going to encourage you, to fulfill God's desires. This in no way means you can't have unbelieving friends or you should cut yourself off from the outside world.

As I told you earlier, I was saved from a life of drugs. This had become my entire life and every person I associated with was a user, a dealer or both. When Jesus became my Lord, my life was literally turned upside down. I didn't want the drugs anymore, but I wanted to see all these acquaintances, receive the freedom I had received.

As you can imagine, I did not always get the warmest reception during the first few weeks of coming into contact with my old unbelieving friends. This was especially true when I did not have any dope to sell or do with them. I knew I could no longer spend time around them, but I did visit some of my old acquaintances. After a few times of sharing my faith with these people, they were convinced I had done one too many trips on LSD. This is the excuse they had to make for my radical change. Though at that moment, none of these people came to the Lord, I know now that a few lives were touched and they later received the Lord.

You need to share your experience of salvation with those unsaved family members and friends in your realm of influence. However, it is just as important for you to closely associate with members of the body of Christ, so that your faith is not quenched through the persecution and denial of others. To discipline your body is to completely identify with Christ and His body.

We have no control over the difficulties we will face and those who persecute us, but we have a responsibility to deny ourselves. The sufferings we experience through the denying of ourselves will take many different forms. Spend an hour in prayer and tell me you don't experience some suffering to the soul. Fast without food and tell me your body and soul are not buffeted. What about when you have to bless someone who did you wrong. I don't know about you, but it hurts my selfish pride. However, the more we buffet our bodies by suffering in the flesh, the greater the release of the Spirit is in our hearts, so that we can do the will of God.

A DISCIPLINED INTAKE OF THE WORD OF GOD

We cannot stop at just presenting our bodies to God, but must continue on to the renewing of our minds. The daily renewal of our minds, which is of necessity to complete the will of God, can only take place as we discipline ourselves in the word of God. A disciple is someone who has committed his life to God's word. Jesus said, **"if you abide in My word, then you are truly disciples of Mine; and you shall know the truth, and the truth shall make you free"** (John 8:31-32) True freedom only comes into our hearts, as we allow the word of God to be securely implanted in us. Knowing the truth does not set us free, but abiding in the word of God on a continual basis brings true liberty.

James 1:21 tells us the type of attitude we must have as we approach the word of God. **"In humility receive the word implanted, which is able to save your souls."** We must put a high value on the word of God. It must become more important to us than our opinions and feelings. Owning a Bible and reading it now and then is not going to renew your mind.

In the 1990's the Barna Research Group took a survey and discovered that among those claiming to be 'born-again Christians': Only 18 percent - less than two of every ten - read the Bible every day. Worst of all, 23 percent - almost one in four professing Christians - say they never read the Word of God. Then we wonder why there is not much difference between the world and the body of Christ!

If you will look at your own life, I am sure you know of areas in your heart, which need the delivering power of God's word. I can tell you that you're only going to experience the living power of God's word, as it is IMPLANTED into your heart.

The Greek word implanted is derived from two other words. *En* means a 'fixed position' and *pho* means 'to puff or to blow up', or to 'grow'. Jesus taught us that the word of God is like a seed planted in the ground.

In the parable of the sower there was only one seed, yet several different types of ground (Mark 4:13-20). The types of grounds are types of hearts. If we want to see the word of God truly grow within us, then we must have a high regard for it. It must be a treasure that we daily seek. As we approach the word of God, it must be with an open heart of humility.

A humble heart, will allow the word to be embedded into your thought processes. This must happen if we want to see the word bear fruit in our lives. As we do this on a consistent basis, our minds will be renewed, emotions stabilized and our will come into alignment with the very thoughts of God and in so doing; we become closely yoked to Him.

If we will daily study God's word, it will work in us. David said that he **'hid God's word in his heart'**. Joshua was commanded to **'meditate upon the word'**, the book of Psalms and Proverbs give multiple references to the necessity of giving the word of God a high priority in our lives. Jesus said that man is not sustained by just natural food, but by the living word of God. We must have a disciplined intake of God's word.

There are several ways in which to study the word of God and I do not have the room nor is it the purpose of this book to cover all of these areas. An excellent book to help you study the Bible is, "How To Read The Bible For All Its Worth", by Gordon D. Fee & Douglas Stuart. I would recommend going to your nearest book store or online and ordering a copy for yourself.

The spiritual discipline I want to focus upon is the discipline of meditating upon the word of God. Once we have discovered the meaning of a text, then we need to allow that portion of scripture to become a part of us. In the Greek language, there are several words used to describe the one word we use for the 'word of God' in the English language.

The two main Greek words used to describe the one English word are *logos* and *rhēma*. There is a debate as to exactly what these two words mean and if there is really that much of a distinction between the two. I have come to the conclusion that there is a difference between the two. In generalities the *logos* is the teaching of the whole Bible. In Hebrews 6:1 the King James Version of the Bible says, "the **doctrines** of Christ", while the New American Standard says, "the elementary **teaching** about the Christ." The word translated into doctrine and teaching is *logos*. The Vines Expository Of Dictionary Words explains the difference between *logos* and *rhēma:*

"The significance of *rhēma* (as distinct from *logos*) is exemplified in the injunction to take "the sword of the Spirit, which is the word of God," Eph. 6:17; here the reference is not to the whole Bible as such, but to the individual scripture which the Spirit brings to our remembrance for use in a time of need, a prerequisite being the regular storing of the mind with Scripture."

We need both the *logos* and *rhēma*. It is important that we regularly study the word of God, yet at the same time we must be open to the Holy Spirit.

The Holy Spirit will breathe upon our hearts to bring the word alive to us, so that it becomes not just a word, but our own personal word. The *rhēma* is a specific word for a specific situation we are facing in real life. It is by the *rhēma* word of God that faith is released so needs will be met, bodies will be healed, lives will be changed and God's divine direction will be given. The *rhēma* word from God will produce a living overcoming faith. However, it is only as we learn to meditate upon the word of God that we are going to see the word become alive in us.

It is this living word, abiding in our hearts that produces the kind of faith, which gives us victory over the world. Christ is more than a book; He is alive. Jesus said that the **"words which I speak they are Spirit and they are Life"**. We must move beyond a mere intellectual study of the word, which is extremely important, to a reality of the Living Word of God working in and through us.

The strongest principle, which shapes and influences a person's thought patterns, is the principle of identification. What ever it is that we most strongly identify with is what we will become like.

Think about this! Does a successful bank robber just start robbing banks? Does the person who has the courage to climb Mt. Everest just wake up one day and do it? No! They spend years thinking and practicing such activity, until they master that which they desire to accomplish. The more they give themselves to such thought patterns, the more strongly their souls become reinforced to be able to successfully do such activities.

We have underestimated the power of meditation. Whether for good or bad, we are molded in our personality and conduct by what we continually think upon. This is the very reason meditation is so important.

The first step in meditation is memorization. The author Dennis Burke says,

> [23] "Some Eastern religions teach that meditation is allowing your mind to become completely blank and empty, but that is far from true biblical meditation. To meditate is to fill your thoughts with the thoughts of God, to be consumed with the things God has said. When you become consumed with what He has said, it becomes effortless to do the things He said to do."

If we want to have true success, then we must see life from God's perspective. This is what God was saying to Joshua. Joshua was confronted with enemies all around, but as He meditated upon what God said, he found the faith, power and wisdom to fulfill God's word. God said that they were to conquer the land. If God said it, then He was providing the grace to accomplish the task; they just had to align their hearts with God's desires.

We must memorize God's word! Faith to overcome is granted only as we hear God's word and become so consumed with what He says that nothing can stop us. Memorization is hiding the word of God in our hearts, so that when the need arises, we will see every situation from God's perspective. We will speak His word, not our fears, insecurities and selfish desires. This is what Paul was saying to the Colossians, when he told them to set their minds on heavenly things. He wasn't telling them to spend time staring into empty space, but to look unto Jesus, the author and finisher of their faith. He was telling them to come into agreement with their Great High Priest by renewing their minds to His word.

This brings us to the next step of meditation, which is confession. In addition to memorization the word meditate means to confess. We must learn to discipline ourselves to say what God's word says. So many believers have learned to believe their circumstances instead of believing the word of God.

The Greek word for confession is *homologia* and it means to say the same as. It is coming into agreement with the High Priest of our confession (Hebrews 3:10). This is not to be a mechanical recitation, but a growing relationship with the word of God. Our faith will grow as we learn to say what God's word says about our circumstances and us. The word of God gives us many great promises that we must embrace with our whole hearts and confess with our mouths. As we do this, we will walk in a greater reality of Christ in us. Faith is learning how to allow Christ to fully live in us. It is a day-by-day walk of continually communicating and abiding in Him, through His words to us.

This brings us to the last step of meditation, which is application. Memorizing the word of God and confessing the word of God, feeds the inner man, so that we can be doers of the word. All successful athletes have daily programs of food and exercise. As a disciple, we must have a daily program to take in the spiritual nutrients we need for running. The end result should be a demonstration of the word in us.

Jesus said that a disciple is one who *bears fruit* (John 15:8). Fruit is something that others will be able to taste. *Our lives are not about what we know, but about what we do.* The word of God must take such deep root in our hearts that we literally become a reflection of His word. Our lives may be the only Bible anyone ever reads.

A Disciplined Life of Prayer

Prayer is not an option for the disciple; it is the very air that he or she breathes. Just as the runner must know how to breathe correctly, so a disciple must learn how to pray.

The disciples asked Jesus to teach them to pray. He taught them to pray by both word and example. We must devote ourselves to a lifestyle of prayer (Colossians 4:2). Devoting ourselves to prayer is not an activity, but a relationship with a Person.

There are many other passages in the Bible, which inform us that God expects us to pray. Richard Foster in his book "The Celebration of Discipline says,"

[24] "All who have walked with God have viewed prayer as the main business of their lives. The words of Mark, "And in the morning, a great while before the day, he arose and went out to a lonely place, and there he prayed." This stands as a commentary on the life-style of Jesus. David's desire for God broke the self-indulgent chains of sleep: "early will I seek Thee" (Ps. 63:1, KJV). When the apostles were tempted to invest their energies in other important and necessary tasks, they determined to give themselves continually to prayer and the ministry of the Word (Acts 6:4). Martin Luther declared, "I have so much business I cannot get on without spending three hours daily in prayer." He held it as a spiritual axiom that "He that has prayed well has studied well." John Wesley said, "God does nothing but in answer to prayer," and backed up his conviction by devoting two hours daily to that sacred exercise."

After I was first saved I desired to know God. I longed for someone to personally disciple me and teach me how to walk as a Christian. In my hunger and thirst for the things of God, I discovered the best Teacher I could ever have received and it was the person of the Holy Spirit. The Holy Spirit became my Teacher and He taught me how to pray.

I along with you, looked at the life of some of these great men and women of God who had gone before, and wondered how I could ever attain to the commitment of prayer, which they displayed. I want to encourage you, that **you can have as deep a walk with God as you desire**. If you too, will give yourself to the Holy Spirit, He will help you in your weakness. Think about it. Do occasional joggers suddenly enter an Olympic marathon? No, they prepare and train themselves over a period of time.

God is not asking you to become a master in prayer overnight. He is asking you to start having a consistent time of prayer everyday. If you will consistently start praying as one of Christ's disciples today, then you can expect to pray with greater authority and spiritual success a year from now than at present. It is time to begin your spiritual journey in prayer, by learning to yield your heart completely to the presence and power of the Holy Spirit.

There are numerous scriptures which teach us about prayer, however the passage which helped me put the missing link of the puzzle together was Romans 8:26. In Romans 8:26 Paul shows us that we cannot pray by ourselves. How many of you have started out in prayer and then five minutes later, you feel as if you are done? There is a longing to pray, but you don't have the will power, the words or the strength to continue. The truth is you don't, this is exactly why Paul said, **"the Spirit...helps our weakness; for we do not know how to pray as we should, but the Spirit Himself intercedes for us..."** The problem is that we have not given the Holy Spirit His rightful place in our prayer lives.

Once again, I must go back to foundational doctrine. The baptism, which we have not discussed, is the 'baptism in the Holy Spirit'. There is a high priority placed upon being filled with the Holy Spirit. It is second only to the emphasis of the work of the Cross in paying for our sins. We cannot neglect nor under-emphasize the importance the Bible places on being filled with the Holy Spirit or baptized in the Holy Spirit.

Whole chapters in John are given to the Holy Spirit, and the book of Acts has been termed the 'Acts of the Holy Spirit.' Jesus told His disciples to not do anything until they were endued with power from on high and Paul in Ephesians 5:18, instructs us to be **"filled with the Spirit"**. It is the Holy Spirit who empowers us with gifts (I Corinthians 12:4-11) and it is by His powerful influence upon our hearts that we are able to display the very fruit of Christ character (Galatians 5:22).

As we are looking at the Spirit and prayer, we need to turn back to the book of Romans. Romans chapter 8 is one of those chapters dedicated to explaining and emphasizing the work of the Holy Spirit. There are 16 direct references made concerning the Spirit in this one chapter. This chapter alone should convince us that without the Holy Spirit, we couldn't live, as Christ would have us to live. The emphasis that I want to place upon this chapter is the needed aid of the Holy Spirit in prayer. Although we have been placed into Christ and adopted as sons and daughters of God, it is the Spirit who aids, so that we can pray as we should.

Jesus has gone away physically as He said He would, however He has not left us without His aid. As we renew our minds with the word of God and allow the Holy Spirit to fill our hearts through prayer, we awaken to the realization that we are seated in Heavenly places with Him. Our spirit, which has been made in His likeness and image, is joined and made one with the very same Spirit, which raised Him from the dead (Romans 8:11). As I began to realize how much I needed the Holy Spirit, then I began to seek to be filled with more of the Holy Spirit.

Jesus promised us that He would baptize us with the Holy Spirit and fire. We see in Acts 2 that the church was brought to birth through the outpouring of the Holy Spirit. From the conception of the body of Christ, it has been empowered with the creativity of the Spirit of life for the fulfilling of its mission. How much more do you think we need the Spirit as we are coming to the end of the age? It is of utmost importance that we tap into the very creative mind of Christ for the fulfilling of His purpose through our lives. It does not matter what we have been called to do we need his creative wisdom and power at work in our lives, businesses, churches actually all that we do.

We must become a Spirit-filled people! I personally do not hold to a traditional Pentecostal theology, which believes the evidence of receiving the baptism in the Holy Spirit is speaking in tongues. I do believe the evidence of the baptism in the Holy Spirit is **the evidence of the power of God** actively working in our lives and within that package will come the availability to speak in tongues. You may say this is simply a play on words, but I believe scripture puts the emphasis on the power of God actively at work in our lives as evidence that we have been baptized in the Holy Spirit. However, the Bible also gives importance to the manifestations of the Spirit at work in our lives (I Corinthians 14:1) and the spiritual power of praying in tongues during our personal devotion to our Father.

I understand this is a controversial subject in some circles. I am okay if you take a different position, but I am writing from my personal experience and clearly Paul's personal experience. He gave a whole chapter to clarify what was then and even now a confusing subject. When you start talking about the Holy Spirit it can be somewhat subjective and everyone experiences Him in varying ways in their lives. I don't propose to clear up the controversy, but I am going to teach you what I see the scriptures teach. The place of the Holy Spirit's active participation is of necessity for each of us to fulfill the will of the Father in the same way that it was for the Pattern Son – Jesus Christ.

It has been my personal experience that, aided by the power of praying in the Spirit, prayer takes on a whole new dimension. Yes we can pray in, by and through the Spirit without praying in tongues, but if you read I Corinthians 14 Paul discusses his use of tongues in both public and private use. Paul, in his discussion with the Corinthian church concerning tongues, told them, **"I thank God, I SPEAK IN TONGUES MORE THAN YOU ALL; however in the church I desire to speak five words with my mind that I may instruct others also"** (I Cor. 14:18-19). (Emphasis Mine)

Paul in no way was teaching against tongues but was putting it in its proper place depending on the context. Paul was not discouraging the Corinthians from speaking in tongues but was instructing them in its proper use. He said in verse 14, **"if I pray in a tongue, my spirit prays, but my mind is unfruitful,"** and in verse 15, **"What is the outcome then? I shall pray with the spirit; and I shall pray with the mind also; I shall sing with the spirit and I shall sing with the mind also."** Praying in tongues is for personal edification, and it is the aiding power of the Holy Spirit helping us in our spiritual walk.

Romans 8:27 says, **"He who searches the hearts knows what the mind of the Spirit is, because He intercedes for the saints ACCORDING TO THE WILL OF GOD"** (Emphasis Mine). The Holy Spirit joins our spirit in praying the very mind of Christ. This is why Paul said, **"I pray with my spirit and I pray with my understanding."** When we pray in tongues, our spirit is being edified and built up through the Holy Spirit.

It is the Holy Spirit who helps us pray accurately. We are limited in our understanding, but the Holy Spirit knows the will of God. Every time you spend 30 minutes praying you are praying out the purpose of God. At the same time, the Holy Spirit will bring revelation to you so you can pray in your understanding. This takes us beyond our limited understanding of prayer so that by the Holy Spirit, we tap into the very mind of Christ. The Holy Spirit will give us answers to problems in our family, work, ministries, cities, etc. We need the revelation of the Spirit of God to see beyond our own understanding since the essence of creativity flows out of our hearts under the inspiration of the Spirit.

Paul in teaching the church in Ephesus about spiritual warfare and prayer told them that **"with all prayer and petition pray at all times in the Spirit"** (Ephesians 5:18). There are many different types of prayer, but it is the aiding power of the Holy Spirit, which is the foundation that helps us to pray. It doesn't matter if we are praying the prayer of supplication, prayer of agreement or are praying the prayer of devotion; we need the Holy Spirit to aid us in prayer.

It is only as we learn how to yield our entire lives to the Holy Spirit, that we are going to have success in prayer. Successful prayer is praying that helps us to walk in and fulfill God's purposes. We can pray all day long, but if we are not praying the will of God, then it is just useless.

Romans 8:27 says **"He who searches the hearts knows what the mind of the Spirit is, because He intercedes for the saints ACCORDING TO THE WILL OF GOD"** (Emphasis Mine). The Holy Spirit joins our spirit in praying the very mind of Christ. This is why Paul said, I pray with my spirit and I pray with my understanding. When we pray in tongues our spirit is being edified and built up through the Holy Spirit.

It is the Holy Spirit who helps and aids us in praying accurately. I don't know about you, but I don't want to waste my time praying for things the Holy Spirit is not leading me to pray about. I John 5:14 say, **"This is the confidence which we have before Him, that, if we ask anything according to His will, He hears us."** I want that full confidence, which comes from the witness of the Holy Spirit in my heart, as I pray according to the word of God. I want to know that I am hitting the target in prayer.

Jesus is our Great High priest interceding for us and as we learn how to yield to His Spirit, we enter into prayer with Him. This is the rest of God. It is a place where we learn to allow the Spirit to pray through us. He knows how and what we need to pray about.

Jesus also knows our weakness in having a prayerful life. He had to exhort His own disciples to tarry in prayer with Him, yet in the end they all fell asleep. This is one of the reasons the Holy Spirit has been sent and that is to help us in our weaknesses. The word 'weaknesses' refers to our inability to produce results because of the limitations imposed on us by our flesh. So the Holy Spirit was sent to help us in our inability to produce results in our own strength. It is only as we learn how to yield our lives to the power of the Holy Spirit, which we can be assured of success in accomplishing the will of God.

There will be times also, that you will need to combine your prayers with fasting. Many view fasting as an attempt to bend God's arm. Fasting is not an attempt to deny ourselves, so that God will be impressed with our dedication. As if our dedication will somehow cause Him to change His mind concerning situations for which we are praying. Fasting is a time to dedicate and open up our hearts to more of the Holy Spirit, so that He can change and align our minds to the will of God.

It is not God who needs to change, it is we, and fasting is a great aid in helping us through this process. It has been my own personal experience that when it comes to fasting, legalism can easily gain a foothold. For far too many believers, fasting becomes nothing more than a lifeless ritual and dead work. However, if we will start off on the right foot with fasting, it will greatly benefit our walk in the Spirit.

Jesus never commanded fasting, but he showed us an example as someone who fasted. At the same time if we look at Jesus own words he teaches that after His resurrection his disciples would fast. We see in Matthew 9:14-15 that **"the disciples of John (the Baptist) came to Him (Jesus), saying, 'Why do we and the Pharisees fast, but Your disciples do not fast?"** (Quotations my words) Jesus answered them by saying, **"The attendants of the bridegroom cannot mourn as long as the bridegroom is with them, can they? But the days will come when the bridegroom is taken away from them, and then they will fast."** The bridegroom was taken from us when He ascended to the right hand of the Father. He has promised His return, but before we see our bridegroom return (Matt. 25:6) we need to be a people who regularly fast. Richard Foster in his book, "Celebration of Discipline" says,

> [25]"The most natural interpretation of the days when Jesus' disciples will fast is the present church age, especially in the light of its intricate connection with Jesus' statement on the new wineskins."

These new wineskins are new hearts changed through the new birth, which are able to hold the new wine of the Holy Spirit. It is regular seasons of prayer and fasting, which will help us remain as flexible wineskins to be able to retain the new wine of the Spirit, continually being poured out in our hearts. Our hearts can become hardened through sin and when this happens, holes open up where the Spirit leaks out of our lives. Regular seasons of fasting are used to help us humble ourselves through repentance and prayer, so that we become soft again. If we will do this on a regular basis, then we will be wineskins that can hold the new wine of the Spirit.

There are many different kinds of fasts and different reasons for which to fast. I want to specifically concentrate on how fasting will aid us in the walk of a Spirit-filled prayer life. When we look at the

Bible and the history of the church prayer and fasting are always found in the lives of those that impacted their generation with the gospel.

When confronting His disciples who had been sleeping while they were supposed to be praying, Jesus said, **"the spirit is willing but the flesh is weak."** Our human weaknesses can be a great hindrance to a prayerful life. Fasting is a key in helping us to press through our own inabilities. At times, we will find it very difficult to overcome certain ingrained habits, which are causing sin to have a place in our lives. The biblical term used when demonic powers have gained a foothold in our lives is called a stronghold. We may study the word and pray, but it just seems impossible to overcome. Another key, to add to our arsenal for bringing ingrained habits under the power of the Spirit is fasting.

Richard Foster says, *"Our human cravings and desires are like a river that tends to overflow its banks; fasting helps keep them in their proper channel."* Biblical fasting is an aid in helping us to buffet our bodies. Fasting shows us clearly that the stomach is not god! By denying our stomachs the right to control us, it brings affliction to our souls. When we lay aside food and put prayer, the study of the word and worshipping God first, it is suffering to the flesh. David said that he afflicted himself with fasting. Isaiah 58:5 says fasting is a time to humble ourselves before God.

Fasting helps us put life in its proper perspective. It is easy to allow nonessentials to take control of our lives. Fasting is a time to take inventory of our lives and put things in their proper order. During a fast we will quickly see the ugliness of any sins we have become accustomed to. It should be a time of repentance and turning away from the strongholds of sin in our hearts. Fasting helps us break out of the ruts of life. By fasting we are laying aside the obstructions of life and are able to more completely focus in upon our true purpose for living, which is God. The goal of fasting is not simply denying our bodies the right to rule us, but it is the building up of our inner man, Christ in us.

Unbelief so easily sets in upon our hearts. This is what Jesus was saying about the lack of power His disciples had, in praying over the young man in Matthew 17:14-21. His disciples wanted to know why they were not seeing results, as they prayed for this young man, who was possessed by a demon. Jesus told them it was because of their unbelief. He then told them the key to seeing powerful prayers answered. It was to add fasting along with their praying. This text has been interpreted in many ways, but I believe the essence of what Jesus is saying, is that those who have a disciplined lifestyle of prayer and fasting, will possess the faith to see powerful prayers answered.

Regular seasons of fasting need to be accompanied with intense prayer and the study of the word. By doing this, you will be able to facilitate a freer flow of the Holy Spirit in you because you have dealt with the sin that causes unbelief. If fasting is accompanied with prayer and the study of the word, it is a means of purifying our faith. Our fasting doesn't move God; it moves us to a place where we can receive from God.

Find some material, which will give you greater insight on the subject, however more than that, just do it. As you learn to fast, you will find that you will possess a greater awareness of the Holy Spirit in your heart as you pray. This will strengthen you to press on beyond your weakness, into a Spirit-led and empowered life. Go beyond what you can do! Press beyond your own natural strength through prayer and you will discover the power you need to run the race before you.

There have been many excellent books written on the spiritual disciplines of the inward life. I have limited my discussion on this subject to the three main disciplines I see in scripture, which are submitting our bodies as a living sacrifice, studying the word of God and prayer. If we don't master our bodies, then we will never accomplish the will of he Father, however it is going to take both a disciplined intake of the word of God and a disciplined life of praying by the Holy Spirit to be able to live a life governed by the Holy Spirit. I am convinced if we will master these three areas then we will experience the power of God and fulfill all that He desires us to accomplish. The tragedy that we face in the church today is that:

[26] "Many Christians know the Scriptures well, but are lacking in the power of God. Others know the power of God, but often drift over into serious error because they do not know the Scriptures, as they should. As we draw near to the close of this age there will be a union of the Word and Spirit that will help to set the church on the proper course with truth, life and power. This will result in the unprecedented release of God's grace, confidence and authority in the church that she will need to accomplish her last day ministry."

A train is a good picture, which we can use to illustrate this truth. The word of God is like the train tracks on which a train runs. The word gives us stability; however the Holy Spirit is the power that runs the engine. Without the word we have no stability, but without the Holy Spirit we will have no power to get to where we are going. There must be a marriage of the Word and Spirit in our lives. If this marriage takes place, we can be assured that our prayers will produce results that move us towards the fulfilling of God's plans for our lives and His church. Also, we will walk in the good works we have been created to accomplish.

PROPHETIC ENCOURAGEMENT ALONG THE WAY

The Holy Spirit has been sent to be with us and work in us. It is His mission to be our Helper. He does not help us fulfill our selfish wants and pleasures, but He is with us to help us run the race set before us. We cannot run in our own strength or by our own ability, we need His help. This help comes to us not only as we pray, but also through the avenue of others.

We all get discouraged and want to quit; this is exactly why it is so important to be a team player. The author of Hebrews in addressing this exact subject says:

"Take care, brethren, lest there should be in any
one of you an evil, unbelieving heart, in falling away
from the living God. But **encourage one another
day after day,** as long as it is still called "Today,"
lest any one of you be hardened by the deceitfulness
of sin" (Hebrews 3:12-13).

Later in this same epistle the author gives a similar exhortation:

"Not forsaking our own assembling together, as is
the habit of some, but **encouraging one another**;
and all the more, as you see the day drawing near"
(Hebrews 10:25).

The main theme that sticks out in these texts is the idea that we
need to be team players, who encourage one another to not quit.
As never before we are living in difficult days (II Timothy 3:1). If
there is anything we all need, it is encouragement to complete and
fulfill the will of God.

Although we live in the most technologically advanced society
ever, we also live in a very pressure filled society. Everyone is
affected by the stress of our times. Whether the source is family
problems, money problems, work or school related pressure we are
all affected by it. We all continually have to fight the pressures of
life, so that we can live the life of faith. This is why fellowship is so
important, because pressure brings fragmentation, if not adequately
addressed.

We have not been created to be under pressure on a continuous
basis. This is why people burn out and have nervous breakdowns.
The pressure has gotten to the point in their lives that they began to
break up, like a plane not able to handle the pressure of high
altitudes. True fellowship with other believers is like a barometer,
that will help us and others detect this fragmentation before it gets
to a critical point. A team player has others in mind. At the point
of exhaustion many times all we need is a cup of water. A cup of

water is equivalent to a refreshing word by the Spirit from a fellow teammate in a time when the pressures of life are exhausting us.

It takes faith to walk in the purposes of God and we are going to need plenty of faith in these difficult days. This is one of the reasons God has put the prophetic gift within His church and that is to encourage us. In I Corinthians 14:3 it tells us that one of the functions of the prophetic ministry is exhortation. Exhortation is the Greek word *paraklēsis.* This word is many times translated as encouragement. The Lexical Aids To The New Testament say: *Paraklēsis* is an exhortation or encouragement for the purpose of strengthening and establishing the believer's faith.

Our walk with God is not isolated from others. When we feel like giving up and everyone will go through seasons during their race, when they will feel like quitting, we need encouragement from teammates.

The scriptures say that sin is deceitful. We don't always see the traps the enemy has laid in our path until it is too late. When that happens we don't need to turn away from others, but we need to learn to lean upon others.

The Holy Spirit will work through others to encourage us to continue to trust God. I can't tell you how many times this has happened in my life. God has used others to speak encouragement to me when I was down. In addition, He has used me to speak encouragement, so that other people's faith could be strengthened when they had been hurt, confused or simply afraid. It seems that this is what Paul was doing to Timothy when he said, "I remind you to kindle afresh the gift of God which is in you through the laying on of my hands" (II Timothy 1:6). The laying on of hands is one of the foundational doctrines of Hebrews 6:1-2. One of the functions of 'laying on of hands' is the impartation of the Holy Spirit into our lives from others.

Prophetic encouragement will keep us from falling down and also help us to get up if we have fallen during the race. We will always face difficulties, which will challenge our faith that is why it is so important to have those people around you who are going to propel you forward with encouragement.

Paul propelled Timothy his apprentice forward with words of encouragement for the fulfilling of his purpose. We also see that during crucial turning points in Paul's ministry the Holy Spirit always encouraged him forward through prophetic encouragement (Acts 21:11). Encouragement is what strengthens our faith in the face of difficulties, so that we continue to go forward towards the goal, no matter what circumstances we are facing.

KEEPING THE PACE

One of the things that many people don't understand about the walk of faith is the necessity of patience. Patience is of the utmost importance to be able to consistently walk in the Spirit led life of faith. In Hebrews 6:12 the author tells us to be **"imitators of those who through** *faith* **and** *patience* **inherited the promises."**

There are several Greek words translated into the one English word patience. One that I want to look at is *hupomonē*. It literally means an abiding under. What is it that the believer is to abide under? We are to consistently abide under the promises of God.

When a runner is running long distances, he doesn't need to be erratic in the speed that he runs. He needs to set a consistent pace and stay with it. Our faith needs consistency. We need to stay under what God has said to us day in and day out. It is consistency that will keep us from going up and down with every differing opinion that comes our way. We need to consistently study the word, pray and sing praises unto God.

Marriage is an excellent picture to observe while discussing the importance of faith and patience. In a marriage the man and woman are a team. What I want you to do is view faith as masculine and patience as feminine, because patience is referred to as her in James 1:4 in the King James Bible. Now when I encounter trials and testing in my life, my wife is there to help me. She is there to support me during difficult times. Patience is there to accomplish the same thing, when my faith comes under attack. Patience becomes a support to under gird my faith. Faith says I have what I believe for, while patience consistently agrees that it is on the way.   Without patience I will lose my pace and tire out during the race, causing me to not reach my goal.

Faith will only produce results if it is mixed with patience. For example, it takes both a man and a woman to have a baby. If faith and patience are not joined together then faith will never produce results.   However, if faith and patience are joined together in intimate union they will bring to birth the purposes of God in your life.

It is the force of patience that keeps us going forward until we reach the finish line. Hebrews 12:1 says to **"run with patience (endurance) the race that is set before you."**   We need to consistently run from a place of rest. As Christ disciples let us live life in union with Him. As we learn to consistently abide in Him, we will have lively, fruitful and overcoming faith. This overcoming faith will see us through until the end, no matter what we face during the race.

CHAPTER 7

PRESSING ON TOWARDS THE GOAL

"I press on toward the goal for the prize of the upward
call of God in Christ Jesus."
Philippians 3:14

Have you have ever watched the ending of a marathon? If you have, then you watched those who desire to win, expend all their energy, yet they're still reaching towards the goal. This is the picture Paul used to describe the life of faith. Starting the race is important, yet only those who finish accomplish their goals. The aged Paul at the end of his life had his final goal set upon one thing and he called it the "**PRIZE OF THE UPWARD CALL of God in Christ Jesus** (Emphasis Mine)."

Paul viewed his heavenly reward directly tied to his obedience to what he had been called to accomplish. This seems to be in alignment with what Paul had formerly said to King Aggrippa by telling him, "**I was not disobedient to the heavenly vision.**" For Paul the 'upward call' was leading a life of obedience to complete the heavenly vision given to him by Christ. We each have a task to accomplish and as disciples we need to see that our reward is directly tied to our obedience in carrying out our God given vision. This should give us the motivation to live as Paul lived and that is a life of pressing on toward the goal.

To reach his goal and complete his heavenly vision was such an important task for Paul that he said, "**I press on in order that I may LAY HOLD OF THAT FOR WHICH I WAS LAID HOLD of by Christ Jesus** (Emphasis Mine)." This was not just a nonchalant task for Paul but the very reason he lived. Paul was consumed with completing the will of God for his life. He was determined to lay hold of all that God had for him. He knew that God had set His hand upon His life and he did not want to stop short of the goal.

The Greek word used for goal in Philippians 3:14 is *skopos* and it is where we derive the English word scope. It means a mark on which to fix the eye and is used metaphorically of an aim. When a marksman uses a scope it is so he can be the most accurate in hitting the desired target. The runners in the Olympics fix their eyes upon the white finish line, or mark. Paul had this same type of mindset. He focused all of his energy towards the prize for completing his God-given task. He was determined, not to let anything stand in his way, which would keep him from reaching forward. Paul couldn't settle for second best.

There is another man we are all familiar with who could not settle for anything short of the plan for which God brought him into this earth to fulfill. He had experienced all of the pleasure and power of the world, but discovered there was something more to life than what we can touch, taste and see. It was said of Moses in Hebrews 11:25-26 that he chose **"rather to endure ill-treatment with the people of God, than to enjoy the passing pleasures of sin; considering the reproach of Christ greater riches than the treasures of Egypt; for HE WAS LOOKING TO THE REWARD"** (Emphasis Mine). Once Moses came to realize his true purpose, he was willing to pay the price. He went from one of the most powerful positions in the world, son of Pharaohs daughter, to one of the lowliest in mans eyes, a shepherd in the wilderness. To be able to fulfill his task he had to look away from his temporal suffering, to his eternal goal.

How many runners do you think concentrate on the exhaustion they are feeling in their bodies? A true runner is concentrating on one thing and it's the finish line! Running is just as much a mental activity as it is a physical one. If you are going to run a long distance, then you have to have the right mindset. You have to keep your mind one-step in front of you, always heading for the finish line. As a disciple, we are going to experience exhaustion, but if we will keep our focus on the finish line and the reward awaiting us, we will discover the supernatural power of hope keeping us in the race until the end.

RUNNING WITH THE END IN VIEW

Eschatology is a theological word we use to describe the doctrine of last things. The last days, end of the age and return of Christ are hot topics in the Christian community and even in the world. There is good reason for this, because the word of God gives attention to this subject.

Numerous authors are identifying what are called the 'signs of the times' and declaring that we are on the precipice of the last days of this age. We need to keep in mind is that we are not the first generation of believers who have thought they would be the generation when Christ would return. It especially becomes an issue when we face hardship during a great turning point in history like the Napoleonic Wars of Europe, the U.S. Civil War, WWI, the Great Depression, WWII with the example of Hitler being an antichrist and even the turmoil during the 1960's drug induced "Sexual Revolution".

Peter in speaking to the first century church said that Christ appeared at the end of times or last days (I Peter 1:20). The early church was actually living in what we would call the 'last days' which started with the first coming, death, resurrection and ascension of Christ. It found its apex at the destruction of the city of Jerusalem in 70 A.D. when the Jewish Temple was destroyed with the ceasing of the sacrifices that has never returned. However, Christ in Matthew 24 did give us specific signs that would precede the completion of the last days, or the end of the age. History is coming to a climax, and we are told to be aware of the conditions in the world, while at the same time expectant concerning the return of Christ.

Peter said, "Know this first of all, that in the last days mockers will come with their mocking, following after their own lusts, and saying, 'Where is the promise of His coming? For ever since the fathers fell asleep, all continues just as it was from the beginning of creation" (II Peter 3:3-4). The world mocks the possibility of

Christ's return, and many even in the church don't give it much thought. I am not recommending fanaticism, but wisdom is a key for the church at the end of this age. Wisdom puts things in their proper perspective. Peter recommended three things in reference to the unveiling, revelation or return of Christ, which are hope, sober mindedness and action (I Peter 1:13).

I have heard many good sermons preached from Philippians chapter 3 but I have heard very few, if any, preach it in the context of which Paul wrote that chapter. The heading for this chapter in the New American Bible says, 'The Goal Of Life'. It is in verse 11 that we see Paul's understanding of this goal when he says, **"that I may attain to the resurrection from the dead."** In the rest of this chapter, Paul is writing from a perspective of resurrection from the dead and the coming judgment at the return of Christ.

In this book we have looked at almost all of the foundational doctrines of Christ, as spoken of in Hebrews 6:1-2. The last two foundational areas, which every disciple needs to be instructed in, are 'resurrection from the dead' and 'eternal judgment'. Paul was always running his race with the end in view. He says in verse 12 of Philippians that I have not **"already obtained it**, (resurrection from the dead vs. 11) **or have already become perfect, but I press on."** (Emphasis Mine) Let us take a look at this word perfect because it is a key to understanding what we are pressing on towards.

When I mention the word perfect many pictures might come to your mind. I think for most of us the word perfect would be defined as something without fault. The concept of biblical perfection doesn't really have anything to do with this type of thinking.

There are many words in the Greek language, which were used to describe perfection, and the majority signifies something reaching its maturity. The Greek word *teleios*, which is translated as perfect, signifies having reached its end, finished, complete, fully grown, fullness and full age. Paul used this word many times. For instance in Romans 12:2 Paul says, **"do not be conformed to this world, but be transformed by the renewing of your mind that you may prove what the will of God is, that which is good and**

acceptable and PERFECT" (Emphasis Mine). There are not three separate wills, but the one will of God, which grows into maturity much in the same way corn grows from a blade, to an ear, to full corn. This word is also used in I Corinthians 13:10: **"when the PERFECT comes, the partial will be done away"** (Emphasis Mine). When Christ returns there is going to be a complete revelation of Him. We won't need the partial spiritual gifts of revelation to give us insight because the complete and perfect revelation will be with us, in Person. "We shall know Him **fully**".

Paul also used this word in Philippians 3:12 and when he did, he was speaking of our final state at the return of Christ. In Philippians 3:20-21 he says:

> vs. 20 "Our citizenship is in heaven, from which also we eagerly wait for a Savior, the Lord Jesus Christ; vs. 21 who will transform the body of our humble state into conformity with the body of His glory..."

Paul had great expectation and insight concerning the return of Christ. He always viewed his present circumstances in light of the final consummation of Christ's return. *He knew the next great event on the calendar of God was Christ's physical return to this earth.* He viewed this as a time when there was going to be a completion to the end of this present age. A time when the followers of Christ would be brought into **the fullness of their salvation**, which is the receiving of a resurrection body just like His.

Salvation is a continuing process and that process reaches its final goal, when we are totally restored to our original condition of being created in God's image spirit, soul and body. Our spirits have already been made in the image and likeness of God. Our souls are continually being transformed to display God's likeness in our personalities and when Christ appears, our bodies will be changed to be just like His resurrection body (I John 3:2, I Corinthians 15:53). It is at Christ's return that we will be brought into the fullness of our salvation. Hebrews 9:28 tells us that: **"He will**

appear a second time, not to bear sin, but to bring salvation to those who are waiting for Him." It is in Romans 8, that we get a glimpse into the display of power, which will be manifested in all the earth at Christ's return. In Romans 8:18-23 Paul the apostle says:

> "vs. 18 For I consider that the sufferings of this present time are not worthy to be compared with the glory that is to be revealed to us. vs. 19 For the anxious longing of the creation waits eagerly for the revealing of the sons of God. vs. 20 For the creation was subjected to futility, not of its own will, but because of Him who subjected it, in hope vs. 21 that the creation itself also will be set free from its slavery to corruption into the freedom of the glory of the children of God. vs. 22 For we know that the whole creation groans and suffers the pains of childbirth together until now. vs. 23 And not only this, but also we ourselves, having the first fruits of the Spirit, even we ourselves grown within ourselves, *waiting eagerly our adoption as sons, the redemption of our body*" (Emphasis Mine).

It is here in this scripture that we get to see, that when Christ returns, His power is going to change our bodies to be like His. At this time, it will also be clearly manifested that we are His children. This is not all that is going to happen! God's glory is not only going to change us, but it is going to cover the earth and His transforming power is going to deliver creation from the curse of sin.

Although we have the Holy Spirit, we are still longing to be clothed with the fullness of the glory of God in an even greater dimension than Adam and his wife in the Garden of Eden possessed. David Pawson in his book, "When Jesus Returns" says,

> [27] "The crowning climax of our restoration will be the gift of a brand new body, uncontaminated by

our sinful past, unlimited in its expression of the
spirit within, unaffected by disease, decay or death."

The Bible says that this will all happen in a flash, just as the
lightning comes from the east, and flashed even to the west, in the
twinkling of an eye, when the last trump blows, Christ will return
and we shall be changed (I Corinthians 15:52).

The change Christ will bring at His return is the very hope of the
Christian's faith. The very hope of our salvation is based upon the
fact that Christ will return to deliver us from this present evil age.
Yes, the body of Christ is to impact this earth with the power of the
gospel, but we are still just pilgrims and aliens in this present age (I
Peter 2:11). The Bible does declare that the righteous will inherit
the earth, but that is only when Christ brings us into the fullness of
His victory at His return. Paul says that at Christ's return He will:

"vs. 7 give relief to you who are afflicted and to us
as well when the Lord Jesus shall be revealed from
heaven with His mighty angels in flaming fire, vs. 8
dealing out retribution to those who do not know
God and to those who do not obey the gospel of
our Lord Jesus. vs. 9 And these will pay the penalty
of eternal destruction, away from the presence of
the Lord and from the glory of His power, vs. 10
when He comes to be glorified in His saints on that
day."

The hope of our salvation is not only based upon the fact of the
redeeming work of Christ through His First Coming, but also His
deliverance, judgment and glory to be revealed at His return.

It is important that we have our hope put in the right places.
Hope is the anchor of our salvation, which keeps us steady through
troubled waters. Paul had to explain this hope to the disciples in
Corinth. While explaining resurrection from the dead, he tells them
"If we have hoped in Christ in this life only, we are of all men

most to be pitied" (I Corinthians 15:19). The New Living Translation says it like this. **"If we have hope in Christ only for this life, we are the most miserable people in the world."** What happens to us if the stock market collapses, our spouse or child dies, we lose our job, we are put in jail or even killed for preaching the gospel? Think about it. If your hope is placed merely on temporal things, it is on shaky ground.

Are you running with the end in view or do you live as if your present circumstances are the ultimate reality? Why live for God, if all we have to look forward to is this life? We are wasting our time and should do what the world does. The world's mentality is, **"Let us feast and get drunk, for tomorrow we die"** (I Corinthians 15:32: NLT). Party up and get all you can get of this life, because when you go in the ground it is all over.

If you look at the book of Ecclesiastes you will see this mentality portrayed as the wisest man that ever lived wrote as one who lived 'under the sun'. As the preacher of vanity, Solomon wrote as a man who was not serving God, but his own self-interest. He looked at life from the viewpoint of an unbeliever and declared all is vanity; therefore get all you can get out of this life because once you're in the ground it is all over. We are not to live our lives 'under the sun' but *'in the Son of God'*. It is only because of Him, that we have a hope, which goes beyond this present evil age and even beyond the grave.

Why live a dedicated life as a disciple of Christ if it doesn't matter? Why suffer in the flesh if I could party up and it wouldn't make a difference in eternity? I have personally had to ask myself these questions. Why should I deny myself a self-indulgent lifestyle? The reason, because life does go beyond the grave and how we live in this life, will be reflected in the life to come! When I discovered this reality, it became a motivation for me to turn away from the temporary pleasures of sin and identify with the Savior.

Each day is a day closer to return of Christ, when we reach our final goal. Paul said in Romans 13:11-14 that our **"salvation is nearer to us than when we believed. The night is almost gone, and the day is at hand...Let us behave properly as in the day, not in carousing and drunkenness, not in sexual**

promiscuity and sensuality, not in strife and jealously. But put on the Lord Jesus Christ, and make no provision for the flesh in regards to its lust"

We are going to experience sufferings in this life, but they are not even worthy to be compared to the glory which will be revealed to us. It is of utmost importance that we view the race we are in now, in the light of the glory, which will be revealed to us. We need to constantly remind ourselves of this hope since Paul said this hope is to be like a helmet affecting our thinking. (I Thess. 5:8)

Our hope must extend beyond this present age or world system. Hope is a firm confident expectation that our future is going to turn out, as God has planned, as we commit ourselves completely to Him. Out of all the people in the world, Christians should have the most positive outlook on life. Not because we are the richest, best looking or most popular, but because no matter what happens in this life, we know that everything is going to be okay. Romans 8:28 has comforted me with eternal hope many times when I felt like giving up. Paul says, **"we know that God causes everything to work together for the good of those who love God and are called according to his purpose for them"** (NLT). When we have our affection on Him who has been raised from the dead we can be confident that He is at work on our behalf. We can confidently say that He is our present help in any time of need.

In Paul's second letter to the Corinthian's we get to see a Paul who opened up and bore his heart. In this epistle he shared his difficulties and heartaches. In this life we are all going to face difficulties and heartaches; however it is how we view them, which will determine our direction. In II Corinthians 4 Paul's main theme is about how it is God's power that makes the difference in our lives when we face trials. Paul ends this chapter showing us the view by which he saw life and the strength, which helped him to run:

> "vs. 16 We are not discouraged, but even though our outer nature suffers decay, our inner self is renewed day after day. vs. 17 For this slight momentary trouble is producing for us an

> everlasting weight of glory that exceeds all measures,
> vs. 18 because we do not fasten our eyes on the
> visible but on the unseen; for the visible things are
> transitory, but the unseen things are everlasting."
> (New Berkeley Bible)

Paul viewed his present circumstances as simply temporary or you might say subject to change. There is an old saying, "This too shall pass." Momentary trouble passes sooner or later! Faith and hope see beyond our present circumstances. When trouble comes our way, it can feel like the end of the world, however I have good news, it is transitory. Your problems are subject to change! Death is not even an ultimate reality for the Christian, but a stepping over into eternal life. Your present body is just a temporary dwelling for the real you. May the real, eternal you, stand up on the inside and declare to your circumstances, "You are not going to have the victory!"

In the opening of the next chapter of II Corinthians, Paul enters right into a discussion about our resurrection bodies. I like the way the Message Bible says it: **"Compared to what's coming, living conditions around here seem like a stopover in an unfinished shack, and we're tired of it! We've been given a glimpse of the real thing, our true home, our resurrection bodies! The Spirit of God wets our appetite by giving us a taste of what's ahead. He puts a little of heaven in our hearts so that we'll never settle for less"** (II Corinthians 5:4-5) For Paul, the end was always in view, because he knew when all was said and done what really mattered was the purpose of God. The apostle John stated this same position by saying "the world is passing away, and also its lust; but **the one who does the will of God abides forever."**

In light of all that we have discussed, let us look back at Philippians 3:14-15 when Paul says, "vs. 14 **I press on toward the goal for the prize of the upward call of God in Christ Jesus. vs. 15 Let us therefore, AS MANY AS ARE PERFECT (MATURE), HAVE THIS ATTITUDE"** (Emphasis Mine). A disciple is one who has learned to run with the end in view, no matter what the cost. It is only those who possess a mature mindset, who will be fit for running when things are not going the way they think they should. Spiritual maturity has nothing to do with physical age, but has everything to do with commitment to the things of God. Maturity is synonymous with being responsible, committed and faithful. You can be 50 years old and still be an immature Christian. However, you can be 15 years old and possess a mature Christian mindset.

Discouragement and unbelief can try to captivate our hearts when our vision doesn't seem to be coming to pass. When purpose is thwarted through adverse circumstances, we don't need to stop, but stretch our faith. The act of 'running' is moving forward, a following on to know the Lord in good times and bad times. To go forward, we will have to follow Paul's advice, which told us to **"forget the things that are behind"**. Don't let failure or success keep you from pressing forward.

You haven't accomplished everything you are supposed to accomplish, until you leave this earth or Jesus returns. We need to be continually going from one degree of strength to another, pressing forward toward the mark for the prize. We cannot stop at the good or acceptable will of God, but must press on to the full maturity of our calling.

Maturing is a process! Is a tree full grown the first day you put it into the ground? Does it bear fruit immediately? No it takes time and it grows in stages. Each stage is beautiful and we will all go through stages in our lives. Our final step of maturity will be when Christ returns, however we are to be pressing forward and maturing everyday. Something that is not growing, changing and maturing is dead!

There are seasons to each of our lives. In certain seasons of my life, I have not always done, what I knew was my ultimate calling. Paul seems to have experienced this same reality. He was called as an apostle. Yet, from the time of his calling, to his release in ministry, was a season of time. It doesn't tell us in the Bible what Paul did during this period of time, but I am sure God was using His circumstances, to prepare and work within him. While God is preparing us, He is working in us, the character traits we will need to fulfill His calling for our lives. I worked as a janitor for many years. It was a season of God's will for my life. I grew through this experience. God worked within me the attitude of a servant and He also freed me from not needing man's approval. Enduring through what seems to be menial activity develops true maturing character within us.

Everyone must go through the wilderness to get to his or her Promised Land. I wish I could tell you there was another way, but there is not. It is as the cowboys in the Wild West used to say, 'bite the bullet'. That means endure and do whatever it takes to reach the goal God has placed before you. Stay under God's promises until you see them finally mature in your life.

There will be times in everyone's life when they are not doing what they desire to do. It is a season, in which God is working in you, His character traits. During periods when you don't think God is working and you are not doing what you desire, whether long or short, never forget that it is only by living within the 'hope of your calling', that you are able to endure with a positive attitude. Keep your vision alive! The only person who can make you quit is yourself. God isn't giving up on you, but calling you to run with the end in view.

WE ARE NOT THOSE WHO DRAW BACK

As the end of the age comes to a close, it is going to be of the utmost importance, to see our present circumstances in the light of eternity. Jesus in speaking about the end of the age clearly tells us that if our eyes do not look beyond our present circumstances, we will have plenty of chances to quit before finishing our goal.

Numerous authors are identifying what are called the 'signs of the times' and declaring that we are on the precipice of the end of this age. One thing that we need to keep in mind is that we are not the first generation of believers who have thought they would be the generation when Christ would return. It especially becomes an issue when we face hardship during a great turning point in history like the Napoleonic Wars of Europe, the U.S. Civil War, WWI, the Great Depression, WWII with the example of Hitler being an antichrist and even the turmoil during the 1960's drug induced "Sexual Revolution".

Peter in speaking to the first century church said that Christ appeared at the end of times or last days (I Peter 1:20). The early church was actually living in what we would call the 'last days' which started with the first coming, death, resurrection and ascension of Christ. It found its apex at the destruction of the city of Jerusalem in 70 A.D. when the Jewish Temple was destroyed with the ceasing of the sacrifices that has never returned. However, Christ in Matthew 24 did give us specific signs that would precede the completion of the last days, or the end of the age. History is coming to a climax, and we are told to be aware of the conditions in the world, while at the same time expectant concerning the return of Christ.

Peter said, "Know this first of all, that in the last days mockers will come with their mocking, following after their own lusts, and saying, 'Where is the promise of His coming? For ever since the fathers fell asleep, all continues just as it was from the beginning of creation" (II Peter 3:3-4). The world mocks the possibility of Christ's return, and many even in the church don't give it much thought. I am not recommending fanaticism, but wisdom is a key for the church at the end of this age. Wisdom puts things in their proper perspective. Peter recommended three things in reference to the unveiling, revelation or return of Christ that are hope, sober mindedness and action (I Peter 1:13). It is my intent to help us have a proper perspective so that we have hope, stay sober minded and are moved to action as we see history unfold.

In advance to the return of Christ, the Bible declares a time of unprecedented trouble. It is in Matthew's gospel, that we find the clearest revelation concerning the future events, which will signal the return of Christ to the earth. In Jesus' response to the question posed by his disciples concerning his return and the end of the age, He says as quoted in the book of Matthew 24: 4-8 that:

> "Vs. 4 See to it that no one misleads you, vs. 5 for many will come in my name, saying, 'I am the Christ,' and will mislead many. vs. 6 And you will be hearing of wars and rumor of wars; see that you

are not frightened, for those things must take place, but that is not the end. Vs. 7 For nation will rise against nation, and kingdom against kingdom, and in various places there will be famines and earthquakes. Vs. 8 But all these things are merely the beginning of birth pangs."

In this portion of Jesus' response to His disciples, we see certain signs specifically mentioned pointing towards Christ's return. I want to focus upon a few of these signs, which are nations rising against nations, earthquakes, pestilence, famines and an increase of knowledge along with travel. The Bible mentions other noteworthy signs for us to observe, but to give adequate attention to these details would be its own book.

The two superpowers Russia and the United States opposed each other throughout the Cold War and everyone was terrified that at any time we could be wiped out by a nuclear exchange of weapons. At the falling of the Berlin Wall in 1992 everyone proclaimed peace and safety in the world as the Bear was declared and the Soviet Union collapsed. However, this could not have been further from the truth. Samuel P. Huntington in his book "The Clash Of Civilizations And The Remaking Of World Order" clearly defines the present state of world affairs.

> [28] "During the Cold War global politics became bipolar and the world was divided into two parts. A group of mostly wealthy and democratic states, led by the United States, was engaged in a pervasive ideological, political, economic, and, at times military competition with a group of somewhat poorer communist societies associated with and led by the Soviet Union."

In the late 1980's when the Soviet Union collapsed this all changed. No longer are the people of the world solely identifying around ideological, political or economic interest. A new added factor that has begun to determine world politics is **culture**.

The Cold War brought an identity crisis to many nations and they are now attempting to answer the most basic questions humans can face: **Who are we?**

> [28] "And they are answering that question in the traditional way human beings have answered it, by reference to the things that mean most to them. People define themselves in terms of ancestry, religion, language, history, values, customs and institutions. They identify with cultural groups: tribes, ethnic groups, religious communities and nations."

What does this have to do with the end of the age? Everything because in the time of the post Cold War we are seeing the words of Jesus come to maturity. He predicted that nation would rise up against nation. The Greek word for nation is *ethnos* and it is where we derive our English word ethnic.

We have always had ethnic conflict, but ethnic conflicts have risen in the world at an alarming rate since the late 1980's. As of early 1993 an estimated 48 ethnic wars were occurring throughout the world, and [28] "164 territorial-ethnic claims and conflicts concerning borders existed in the former Soviet Union, of which 30 had involved some form of armed conflict."

In the United States, we are most familiar with the ethnic wars with which we have been directly involved in like Somalia, Bosnia, Kosovo, Ireland and Israel. However, almost every nation is facing some type of ethnic conflict. North America has its own forms of ethnic conflict, which are usually played out in the political realm, such as Quebec succession. However, on occasion it does move into armed confrontations such as the L.A. Riots and Chiapas Indians of Mexico. We are all familiar with the terrorist attacks of 9/11, which is surely a cultural conflict.

This is only one sign, which is obviously pointing to Christ's return, not to mention the increase of earthquakes and famines. The World Almanac tells us that there were only 21 earthquakes of major strength between the years 1000 and 1800. But between 1800 and 1900 there were 18 major earthquakes. In the next 50 years, between 1900 and 1950, there were 33 major quakes, and between 1950 and 1991 there were 93 major earthquakes, almost tripling the number of the previous half century, and claiming the lives of 1.3 million people around the world. This is not to mention the 9.0 magnitude earthquake in December 2006 setting off a major tsunami killing over 150,000 people on the coastline of 11 Indian Ocean countries.

At the same time throughout the 1990's more than 100 million children died from illness and starvation. While some famines are caused by drought or other-so-called natural disasters, an equal amount is caused through war, embargoes and government corruption.

In other passages, Jesus mentions that pestilence will also greatly increase. We have the most advanced medicine in the history of the world, but instead of fading, the cases of infectious diseases have skyrocketed throughout the 90's. Dr. Sherwin Nuland, in his best selling book, "How We Die," laments, "Medicine's purported triumph over infectious disease has become an illusion. There are certain countries in Sub Sahara Africa, which are being ravaged by Aids. At the same time, the emergence of bacteria strains that cannot be killed by the current arsenal of antibiotics is making once conquered diseases like tuberculosis; pneumonia, meningitis and staph infections become unstoppable". There is also a growing concern over the Bird Flu, Swine Flu, Sars and the Ebola virus. This is not to mention the pestilence sweeping through the animal world. Millions of cattle and sheep during the winter and spring of 2001 had to be killed in Europe because of mad cow disease and the less deadly, but more rapidly spreading foot and mouth disease.

The book of Daniel mentions other signs prior to the 'time of the end'. He said, **"many will rush here and there, and knowledge will increase"** (Daniel 12:4: NLT). The rapid increase of travel and learning are simply accelerating the calamities of the last days. Since the 1900's, man has seen an exponential increase in learning and travel. These two areas have literally excelled beyond our imagination. We have gone from horses, slow trains and ships, to jet planes, cars and super trains. At the same time we have entered into the 'Information Revolution'. The increase of information is growing exponentially day-by-day. With the creation of the Internet, societies and people are being interconnected around the globe. Our ability to travel quickly and transfer information fast is having both a positive and negative effect worldwide.

Paul fittingly termed Christ's First Coming as the **'fullness of times**.' His arrival was timed perfectly! Christ stepped into time during the rule of the Roman Empire. This was during a period when there was basically a one-world government connecting different peoples together and an adequate road system by which they could easily travel. These circumstances greatly aided the quick spread of the gospel during the first 200 years of the church.

We have never been in a greater position to reach the peoples of the world with the gospel than today. We are in the midst of becoming the most interconnected generation that has ever lived. We need to use our present circumstances in these last days for the spreading of the gospel. The church doesn't need to go hide in a cave, but we need to take advantage of these circumstances that God has allowed to happen.

Yes, there are also negative aspects of our ability to travel quickly and distribute information at the touch of a button. In the last days, the gospel will not only spread quickly, but the spread of disease and fear will move from one place to the other in just a short span of time. We can spread a disease from one continent to the other in an hour's time. Someone gets on a plane in the Democratic Republic of Congo, which was formerly Zaire and can land in New York twelve hours later carrying the deadly Ebola virus. Thank God for news, this keeps us up to date, but with our constant barrage of news, fear and panic, can also spread at an alarming rate. Jesus said men's hearts would be failing them because of what they are going to be seeing coming upon the earth.

How do you think they are going to be able to see everything? Our information society will make it possible to watch it all happen!

As Christ's disciples, we must not allow such catastrophes to cause fear nor alarm. It is important to understand the purpose for which Jesus gave us signs. It was not so we could argue dates of His return or fight about our interpretation of the book of Revelation, but so we could avoid the danger of the last days. The greatest danger that we will face is the temptation to give up and quit. Matthew 24:11-13 says:

> vs. 11 And many false prophets will arise, and will mislead many. vs. 12 And because lawlessness is increased, most peoples love will grow cold. vs. 13 But the one who endures to the end, he shall be saved."

Though many will be fainting because of the difficulties coming upon the earth, we must not be those who draw back. In the day of adversity we must continue to run. There is an old saying which says, "When the going gets tough, the tough keep going."

It is of utmost importance that we view the difficulties of the last days, as nothing more than birth pangs and the beginning of a new age. Paul said that, **"the whole creation groans and suffers the pains of childbirth together."** The signs of the last days are simply the world experiencing the pains of childbirth. In childbirth, the contractions begin suddenly, but are spread out between intervals of time. When it is time to give birth, the contractions become intense and more frequent. The signs of the end of the age have greatly increased since the early 1900's.

> [29] "During the "transition" stage when the baby is entering the birth canal, the mother usually goes through severe disorientation. Physicians specializing in natural childbirth have found that it helps immensely for the mother to have a 'focal point' on which to

concentrate during this time. It has never been more critical for the church to concentrate with discipline and determination upon her 'focal point,' the ultimate purpose of God, that he might bring many new sons to birth."

Jesus said that the signals of the end of the age would be accompanied by a great harvest: **"The gospel of the kingdom shall be preached in the whole world for a witness to all nations, and then the end shall come."** Disciples will not only stand firm until the end, but they will be the harvesters in the last great harvest of souls before Jesus returns. *Times of difficulty and pressure are not times when the church should retreat, but press forward focusing its entire attention on fulfilling the purpose of God.*

A church purified under pressure becomes a church, which displays the glory of God. This has been confirmed throughout history and if we look just at the example of China during the 1990's and early 2000's it can be seen that persecution cannot stop the true church. It only serves to propel true disciples in fulfilling their purpose by using their individual gifts in fulfilling the Great Commission.

The true church has always grown and matured under pressure. God is bringing His church to a place of maturity. His ultimate desire is that we will grow into the **"measure of the stature which belongs to the fullness of Christ"** (Ephesians 4:13). The church will be matured and completed as a bride is presented to her bridegroom (Ephesians 5:27; Matt. 25:10). However, the maturing process can only be completed as the pressures are applied to reveal and mature our true character.

Paul also talked about **"the fullness of the nations"** coming to Christ (Romans 11:25). This gospel must go to every tribe, tongue and nation upon the face of the earth. The focus of the church must not just be inward inspection, but a clear determined focus on reaping a harvest of souls. Jesus said the harvest is the end of the age (Matthew 13:39). Harvesting is hard work, but it brings great rewards. Harvesters don't sit down, but roll up their sleeves and press towards the reaping of every part of the field. As disciples we have been called to harvest so lift up your heads, the fields of the nations are whitened and you are one of the reapers.

ONLY WINNERS RECEIVE REWARDS

There is a story about three boys.

> [30] "The snow covered the ground, and three young boys were playing in it. A man said to them, "Would you like to try to race, with the promise of a prize for the winner?"
>
> The boys agreed, and the man told them that his race was to be different. "I will go to the other side of the field," he said, "and when I give you the signal, you will start to run. The one whose footsteps are the straightest in the snow will be the winner.'
>
> As the race started, the first boy began looking at his feet to see if his steps were straight. The second boy kept looking at his companions to see what they were doing; but the third boy just ran on with his eyes fixed on the man on the other side of the field.
>
> The third boy was the winner, for his footsteps were straight in the snow. He had kept his eyes on the goal ahead of him."

The race of faith has a lot of resemblance to this story. The race of faith is won by staying focused with undistracted attention fixed on Christ until we reach our goal and receive our reward.

There is a chiding little rhyme children use on playgrounds all over America. "Winners keepers, losers weepers." Jesus in many of his parables concerning His return taught this exact principle. At His return He is not only going to resurrect the righteous, but He is also going to judge and reward them for how they ran their race. In the book of Matthew just after Jesus finished explaining to His disciples about the signs preceding His return, He shares with them several parables. The first parable is in Matthew 24:42-51. In this parable there is a slave who has been left in charge of the household while his master was away. In this story, there is a call to holiness and faithful obedience in carrying out their assignment. Jesus said:

> "vs. 46 If the master returns and finds that servant has done a good job, there will be a reward (NLT). vs. 47 Truly I say to you, that he will put him in charge of all his possessions. vs. 48 But if that evil slave says in his heart, 'My master is not coming for a long time,' vs. 49 and shall begin to beat his fellow slaves and eat and drink with the drunkards; vs. 50 the master of that slave will come on a day when he does not expect him and at an hour which he does not know, vs. 51 and shall severely scourge him and assign him a place with the hypocrites; weeping shall be there and the gnashing of teeth."

We see in this parable, a reward for faithfully carrying out the assignment given and punishment for allowing corrupt activity to crowd out their vision for doing what God desires. Paul in addressing the church in Thessalonica spoke in a very similar manner (I Thess. 5:3-8).

In Matthew 25:14-30 Jesus tells another parable, which has been popularly termed the 'parable of the talents.' In this parable, Jesus tells the story about a man who went on a journey and entrusted his slaves with differing amounts of money. **"He gave five bags of gold to one, two bags of gold to another, and one bag of gold to the last - dividing it in proportion to their abilities."** Upon his return, the master judged his slaves and rewarded them according to their faithful service. He expected a return on his investment of money. The one, who was afraid to take a risk, was called unfaithful and was punished accordingly. Again, the concept of reward and loss is taught in the context of the return of Christ.

God has invested in each one of our lives. He has entrusted us with His gifts and we must faithfully put them into use. This is exactly the reason Paul encourages us to run in such a way that we may win. He knew that at the end of our race we were going to be judged. II Corinthians 5:10 specifically mentions the 'judgment seat of Christ.' Paul compared the coming 'judgment seat of Christ' to the ancient seat in Greece where the judge gave awards to the winner of the games.

When the Grecian games were celebrated, running was one of the main events. At a race, a wreath of pine or ivy was hung at the goal and awarded to the victor. This was the beginning of our present day World Olympic competitions. Just as these athletes, were and still are rewarded for their performance, so Christ as the Judge will award His own for their faithful service to Him.

We can never underestimate the motivating power of a reward! How many athletes do you know who train hours a day, discipline their bodies and keep strict eating habits, but expect to receive nothing for their hard work? Think about the businessman who spends an extra 20 hours a week to complete a large project and works on a fixed salary. Do you think his motivation and determination to complete the project would greatly increase if he knew that he would get a large bonus for a job well done? Reward is also a motivating factor in the disciple's life!

As a new believer, we learn that our salvation is based upon faith in Christ alone. As stated earlier in this book 'repentance from dead works' teaches us that there is no amount of religious work we can do, to gain God's favor because it is by grace through faith that we are saved. However, we must balance this view with the reality of 'eternal judgment'. The aspect of eternal judgment, which affects every Christian, is the judgment seat of Christ. It is at the judgment seat of Christ that we will be rewarded for our good works. We have been created to do good works and we will be rewarded for our faithful obedience to complete them day-by-day.

The judgment seat of Christ is not a judgment to determine whether we spend eternity in heaven or hell. The judgment of our eternal salvation is made before we leave our present body and it is based on our acceptance or rejection of Christ. **At the judgment**

seat of Christ, we will have to give an account for what we have done with our time, money, relationships, gifts, possessions, bodies, occupations and etc.

Winning is everything! However, in this race we are not judged and rewarded by our performance in comparison to other people's performance. We are judged by our faithfulness and obedience to God's calling for our own personal lives.

Peter tells us that each person will be judged impartially according to his or her works (I Peter 1:17). You are going to be judged for your personal performance in the race of faith. This takes the sweat out of trying to measure up to others. I don't have to be like Paul the apostle or any other Christian leader, but I can be the best me that there ever has been. You have been specifically created to fulfill a specific purpose.

Let's take a closer look at the parable of the talents. In this parable the master gave each of his slaves **'according to their ability'**. God is not asking anyone to do something they have no ability to accomplish. Can you imagine asking your two-year-old son to paint the house and mow the lawn? That is not within his realm of ability. God is not holding us accountable for things outside of our ability or our sphere of influence. He has gifted each of us, with the ability to accomplish our purpose and has given us a sphere of influence or as previously stated our measure of rule, so that we can work out our particular calling. We are going to be held accountable for what we have been given. This is exactly why it is so important to not think more highly of ourselves than we should or to allow fear and insecurity to cause us to bury our abilities.

Let's put this down on a practical level. I have known many people in my life miss God's purpose for their lives. In reality they have missed life all together, because they were following a dream outside of their realm of God given ability.

I had a friend I met named James. He was a nice guy, yet as I became more familiar with him, I could tell he was a little slow. He was a slow learner and he just did things slow. James' dream was to be a pastor. James had a big heart, but he did not have the capacity to be the key leader over a congregation. That wasn't the only problem. During this period that I knew him, he never held a job for any length of time. In addition, he was always having conflict with others and from his viewpoint it was never his fault.

I watched this man as he came in and out of my life practically never accomplish anything of lasting value over a 10-year span. I am in no way putting James down, but he had not been given the talent to fulfill the dream he was pursuing. That is not the real tragedy. The real tragedy is that James wanted to live the life of someone who had four talents when he only had two. He couldn't assess himself with accuracy and humility.

If James could have been faithful he could have made a great assistant to the leader of a congregation. However, he viewed success as being the leader of a church instead of simply using the talent he had been given, so that he could accomplish his calling. He is over 50 at the writing of this book and still in the same spot. Far too many Christians live this kind of life! Instead of taking what they have been given and using it to the best of their God-given ability, they bury it. They become paralyzed in a false hope, built upon an inflated opinion of themselves! Instead of working toward the fulfillment of a vision, they are always living in a dream world and never really accomplishing anything.

Over the years I have also met others who have been given 4 talents and walk around acting like they only have one. This type of person has allowed insecurity and the fear of man keep them from releasing and increasing their God-given ability. There are also far too many of these types of people, who have allowed the fear of failure and the opinion of man paralyze them from releasing the treasure that lies within them. Proverbs says, the fear of man is a snare and Jesus said don't worry about what man thinks of you, but be concerned about what I think of you (My paraphrase). When it is all said and done it doesn't matter what man thinks, but what God thinks.

In the body of Christ we are not competing against one another or at least we are not supposed to be. We are supposed to be a team helping one another and spurring one another on to the finish line. However, when we reach the finish line and are resurrected at Christ's return, *we will stand alone*, at the judgment seat of Christ.

"We must all appear before the judgment seat of Christ, that each one may be recompensed for his deeds in the body, according to what he has done, whether good or bad." **(II Corinthians 5:10)**

I am not going to be judged for your works, but mine. Not your spiritual mentor, mother nor any other person is going to stand beside you holding your hand at the judgment seat of Christ. You will stand naked and open before God, giving an account concerning your faithful obedience to His will. You won't be able to blame anyone, but yourself.

I have come to realize that when all is said and done, I have one person to answer to and that is God. When I stand before Him, I alone will bear the brunt of my obedience or disobedience. I won't be able to say, well so and so, told me to do it or so and so, told me not to do it. The final response to do or not do something is up to me and I can blame no one else for my words, actions or conduct.

At the end of the parable of the talents in Matthew 25:30 the expression **"outer darkness"** occurs along with **"weeping and gnashing of teeth."** The Greek scholar Spiros Zodhiates says in this text **"outer darkness"** does not mean Gehenna, the place of burning for unbelievers.

> [31] "It is applied to believers who neglected to exercise their God-given talents. It is a place of far less rewards for the servants who proved themselves less diligent than those who used and exercised their talents to the fullest."

The expression **"weeping and gnashing of teeth"** demonstrates disappointment and anger at oneself for missed opportunities. We have all experienced this type of regret when a prime opportunity has passed us by. This is where the expression "I could kick myself" comes from. The Lord wanted to teach that, after death, we couldn't go back and do it over.

This is why it is so important to serve Him according to our God-given opportunities today. Ephesians 5:15-17 tells us to "vs.

15 **look carefully how you walk, not as unwise men, but as wise,** vs. 16 **making the most of your time, because the days are evil.** vs. 17 **So then do not be foolish, but understand what the will of the Lord is.**"

The judgment seat of Christ is going to be a consuming fire, which will lay the foundations of our lives bare. You may have read this book and feel as if you have already wasted too much time and that your destiny has already passed you by. I hope to encourage you, by showing you that it is never too late for you to surrender all to God.

There are numerous examples in the Bible of God using people who had been failures, murders, adulterers, and the list could go on. If you have stumbled and fallen, God is not giving up on you, so don't give up on yourself. God is the God of all hope and restoration. We see in the book of Hosea that God extended His hand of mercy to the disobedient and rebellious nation of Israel, who had become entangled in sin.

In Hosea 2:15 it says that God opened, **"the valley of Achor as a door of hope"**, to the children of Israel in their state of rebellion and failure. This hope, which comes from walking through the valley of Achor, is still an open door. It is open for all who have come to an end of themselves and are ready to stand up to walk in God's will.

Historically, the 'valley of Achor' was a place of God's fiery judgment. It is in the book of Joshua that this place is first mentioned. In Joshua chapter 7, just after the children of Israel had defeated the city of Jericho, they then were defeated by the much smaller city of Ai.

In searching for the answer to why they had failed to conquer the city of Ai, they discovered a man by the name of Achan, who had rebelled against the command of God to not take any of the spoils of Jericho. He had taken what was forbidden to take and buried the spoils in the ground under his tent. Joshua and all Israel brought Achan, his family and all of his belongings to the valley of Achor. They stoned them in the valley and burned them with fire.

This same valley of Achor is the door of hope Hosea told Israel that God had opened for them.   How could a place of fiery judgment also be a place of hope?   It is because, through His fiery judgment, God was going to consume that which was keeping Israel back from a complete dedication to His will!   God uses fire to consume the debris, which has gotten in our pathway.

Jesus spoke in a similar manner in the parable about the prodigal son. The prodigal was a son who received his inheritance; yet he allowed his own foolish decisions and lustful passions cause him to waste all that he had, with nothing to show.   He never stopped being a son, even when he was in the pigpen. He paid a dear price for his rebellion, yet when he finally came to his senses and returned home, his father's love accepted him back. What finally brought this man to his senses? This man was brought to his knees while feeding swine far away from home. He finally started reaping what he had sown in his life! He was experiencing the fire of God's *present day judgment.* As his life lay in ashes, he finally realized the dire consequences, resulting from his self-willed rebellion.

God's fire is pictured in scripture as His divine judgments, testing the quality of believer's lives. Paul in I Corinthians 3:13 talks about what is going to happen at the judgment seat of Christ. "Vs. **13 each man's work will become evident; for the day will show it, because it will be revealed by fire; and the fire will itself test the quality of each man's work. vs. 14 If any man's work which he has built upon it remains, he shall receive a reward. vs. 15 If any man's work is burned up, he shall suffer loss; but he himself shall be saved, yet so as through fire."** The fire of God is going to reveal the quality of our work. When we do finally appear before the judgment seat of Christ, it is going to be a time when what we have done will be tested and revealed by fire. It is not how much we do that matters. What matters is that we are doing what we are supposed to be doing. Quality, not quantity is the real issue.

There is going to be a specific time when we will be judged, however there is an ongoing *present day judgment* which the author of Hebrews calls discipline. Hebrews chapter 12 begins by talking about the race we are running, the discipline we need while running and ends with the statement, **"our God is a consuming fire."** In Hebrews 12:5-8 we are exhorted to not **"ignore it when the Lord disciplines...and don't be discouraged when He corrects...For the Lord disciplines those He loves and He punishes those He accepts as His children"** (NLT).

God's discipline is meant to cut us off from the things that are keeping us from running a straight course. The Message Translation says that through discipline **"God is educating us; that's why we shouldn't quit. It's like training from a coach which has the purpose of strengthening us to finish the race."** It is not always pleasant, but if we will take heed, it will save us a lot of time, keeping us out of the ditches and pigpens of this world.

The present day judgment of God is administered in two main ways. We can be disciplined through the instruction of the word of God or through our circumstances brought upon us by foolish decisions. When we experience adverse circumstances, it is a time to take inventory of our lives and adjust our course from any bad decisions we have made. This is what happened to the prodigal son. He finally came to a place where he examined his life!

Paul in speaking about partaking of the Lord's Supper gave similar instruction. He said, that when we eat the bread and drink the cup, it should be a time of examining our lives (I Cor. 11:28-32). He says that if we will examine and judge ourselves, then we will not be judged by the Lord. However, if we refuse to adjust and correct our course when needed, then the Lord will discipline us!

God's discipline is allowing us to reap what we have sown. If we are self-willed and rebellious, refusing to listen to His instruction, then He will stand back and let us go into the ditches of life. He will allow us to be overtaken by our disobedience, until we repent and cry out for His mercy, much in the same way as the prodigal son.

God's purpose behind His fiery discipline is to bring us back to being established on the foundation of Christ. It is a burning up of the debris and sin, which tries to entangle us. At the same time, it is meant to purify our purpose, so that we spend our time doing the right thing. The fire only burns up that which is useless and of no eternal value in our lives. God allows this to happen because He loves us and desires to see us be all that we can be.

It is never too late to dedicate your life to God. Maybe you have let things stand in the pathway of your purpose. You may say, 'I am too old', 'I have sinned too much', 'I have made too many mistakes' or 'I am just a failure'. Don't give up! If you will live the rest of your life faithfully pursuing God, you will be rewarded. You can't change yesterday, but you can affect your tomorrow.

Stand up on your feet and rededicate your life! Just as God opened up a door of hope to the children of Israel who had done everything wrong, He stands before you today with an open door of hope. It is time to walk through that door and get on with your life.

God has given each one of us individual abilities so that we can be a part of helping in completing the Great Commission. He has not left out anyone. There are no spare parts in the body of Christ. God has made no duplicates; you are an original created for a specific purpose.

Find your place in the body of Christ and begin to pursue with diligence the plan and purpose of God. Be a team player and pull your weight by being a disciple. You are a valuable part and no one can take your place on the team. You may forfeit your place on the team with continued acts of sin, but if you are really a part of the team you will listen to your teammates and allow them to restore you so that you can become a vital part again.

Discipleship is about being a faithful follower of Christ, completing His will and helping others to do the same. Don't you want to hear, **"Well done good and faithful servant"**, when you get to the end of your race? Run like one who has made up his mind to win, no matter what the cost. There will be many obstacles and reasons to give up along the way, however we must never forget that the prize is going to be so rewarding that the hard work along the way will be worth it all. I want to end with the exhortation of Paul the apostle, "RUN IN SUCH A WAY THAT YOU MAY WIN."

Bibliography

1. Dr. Jack Deere, "A Passion For Jesus" (Orlando, Florida: Creation House, 1993), Pg. 10.

2. Eugene Peterson, "A Long Obedience In The Same Direction", (Intervarsity Press, 1980), Pg. 16.

3. Charles Stanley, "Overcoming The Enemy"(Nashville, Tennessee: Thomson Nelson, 1997), Pg. 7.

4. Francis Frangipane, "The Three Battlegrounds" (Cedar Rapids, IowaArrow Publications, 1989), Pg. 12.

5. William Barclay, Flesh and Spirit. (Bloomsbury Street London: SCM Press Ltd., 1962), Pg. 20.

6. Bob Mumford, "The Purpose Of Temptation" (North Brunswick, New Jersey: Bride-Logos, 1996), Pg. 114.

7. Richard Booker, "The Miracle Of The Scarlet Thread" (Shippensburg, PA: Destiny Image), Pg. 136

8. Rick Joyner, "There Were Two Trees In The Garden"(Charlotte, NC: Morning Star Publications), Pg. 133.

9. Rick Joyner, "There Were Two Trees In The Garden" (Charlotte, NC: Morning Star Publications), Pg. 161.

11. Frank Viola, "Rethinking The Wineskin" (Present Testimony Ministry), Pg. 44

12. George Barna, "The Power Of Vision" (Ventura, California: Regal Books), Pg. 11.

13. Myles Munroe, "Releasing Your Potential" (Shippensburg, PA: Destiny Image Publishers), Pg. 50.

14. Rick Joyner, "Leadership, Management" (Charlotte, North Carolina: Morning Star Publications), Pg. 161

15. William H. Cook, "Success, Motivation and the Scriptures" (Broadman & Holman Publishers), Pg 55.

16. A Treasury of Bible Illustrations, AMG International Inc. Pg. 319.

17. Bob Mumford, "The Purpose Of Temptation" (North Brunswick, NJ: Bridge-Logos), Pg. 115.

18. Dr. Michael Brown, "Go And Sin No More" (Ventura, California: Regal Books), Pg. 203.

19. Kelly Varner, "Prevail A Handbook For The Overcomer" (Shippensburg, PA: Destiny Image), Pg. 99.

20. Andrew Murray, "Holiest Of All" (New Kensington, PA: Whitaker House), Pg. 148.

21. V. Ramond Edman, "The Disciplines Of Life", Pg. 46.

22. Rick Joyner, "The Journey Begins" (Charlotte, NC: Morning Star Publications), Pg. 14.

23. Dennis Burke, "How To Meditate On God's Word" (Tulsa, OK: Harrison House), Pg. 6.

24. Richard Foster, "Celebration of Discipline" (New York, NY: Harper and Row), Pg. 30-31.

25. Richard Foster, "Celebration of Discipline" (New York, NY: Harper and Row) Pg 120.

26. Rick Joyner, "The Scriptures And The Power Of God" (Charlotte, NC: Journal Vol. 3 No. 3), Pg. 50.

27. David Pawson, "When Jesus Returns" (London, England: Hodder & Stoughton), Pg. 38.

28. Samuel P. Huntington, "The Clash Of Civilizations And The Remaking Of World Order" (New York, NY: Touchstone), Pg. 35 36.

29. Rick Joyner, "The Harvest", (Charlotte, NC: Morning Star Publications), Pg. 34.

30. A Treasury Of Bible Illustrations, AMG International Inc. P g. 84.

31. Spiros Zodiates, "The Hebrew Greek Study Bible". Pg 1368.